STRANGE ENCOUNTERS

Tales Of A Renegade Naturalist

TABLE OF CONTENTS

FOREWORD

"I give up. My father will never stop traveling," Nancy, my daughter, said over the phone to my wife. Nancy was trying to locate me. Like most of our relatives and friends, her first question when she called was "where are you?" Traveling has been part of my life. I have worked for many decades trying to understand how nature works and trying to help solve environmental problems. I have tried to live a reasonable life, to bring my kids up well and to get along as best I could in the world. I have tried to have fun along the way. In the process of doing my work and living my life, I had some curious experiences. Often, the simplest facts that I thought would be easiest to find eluded me. Sometimes people would get into debates and arguments that didn't seem to make sense and to hate each other unnecessarily. Sometimes people did things that were funny. I learned a lot from the human side of nature and wilderness.

These experiences raise several questions. What can people expect of science when it is applied to the world immediately around them? What is the best that such science can do? What is it realistic to expect of such a science when it is done by human beings, with all our failings as well as our strengths? What is reasonable for such a science, and the scientists, to expect from the people, governments and other institutions that are supposed to oversee, manage properly, and improve our surroundings?

When I give public talks, I often use one or two of these stories. People seem to enjoy them, and each has a point. Sometimes the point has to do with our inability to think clearly, and the peculiar problems this gets us into. This book contains some of my stories.

A change is taking place in our myths about nature - in our nature knowledge - with immense implications for ourselves and life on the Earth. I am not talking about the Armageddon feared from human destruction of the environment - that is another story, related and unrelated. This is a change taking place subtly but definitely, as soft as a kitten but with the momentum of an elephant. It is perhaps the greatest change in human perception of nature and our role in nature in the last four thousand years --- since the beginning of the great myths of western civilization about the balance of nature. The change confuses us and leads to poignant and humorous incidences that are the symptoms of the change --- the inflamed pustules on our body of nature-knowledge. This change has taken place during my lifetime, from the 1960s to the present. Working in ecology, I saw this change affect how people acted and how their actions were perceived—not just regarding the environment, but about how people have been interacting in recent years. The change is best told in the stories that happened to me or to one of my friends, beginning with the story of Maggie's bend and the difference between how that situation was seen and solved and the old self-righteous perception of people's role in nature.

CHAPTER 1

Maggie's Bend

Maggie's Bend was a whorehouse in Koskoosia, Idaho, when the Feds arrived in town and announced that they were adding the part of the Clearwater River that flowed through the town to the United States Wild and Scenic Rivers System. They were condemning and purchasing private land along the river, including the part of Koskoosia where Maggie's Bend stood. At the time, prostitution was legal in Idaho, and the Feds -- in this case the U. S. Forest Service -- had to establish a fair market value for the property.

Maggie's Bend was owned by a fellow known as Whorehouse Jack. Nobody knew his complete name, or real name for that matter. His house contained 19 fully carpeted bedrooms, and was worth quite a lot, especially compared to the usual houses in this part of Idaho. The facility presented the Forest Service with a special dilemma: how to arrive at a fair market value for the business, so that Whorehouse Jack could be compensated? The Forest Service had to establish the value of the capital investment and the value of the ongoing business, based on present income and expenses, and past and potential future profits.

The straightforward method, visiting and using the facilities and determining their value firsthand, or watching the goings-on and the exchange of funds, wasn't quite the right approach for an employee of the U. S. Forest Service. What to do?

Some locals suggested that the house ought be kept within the wilderness system anyway, since it met with their ideas of wild and scenic, and would probably be welcome to many of the men, if not the women, who struggled down the Clearwater through the wilderness until they reached Koskoosia, which was near the southern end of the wilderness area to be set aside.

The Supervisor of the Clearwater National Forest figured out a solution. He visited the laundry facilities of Maggie's Bend and estimated the level of current business by counting the number of towels washed each day. A clean solution to a touchy situation. Of course, he had to know the number of towels used per transaction. This number would likely vary with each transaction, so the ratio would have an average value and some variation. My sources do not tell me how the Supervisor arrived at this ratio, but we can assume that he did so by some legitimate means.

The forest Supervisor's solution to Maggie's Bend has a certain charm to it. It is especially charming to me, because I have worked my professional life --50 years -- to try to help improve the environment and to understand how nature works. Often, I find that people become so upset by the mistakes and failures in our attempts to conserve nature that they become puritanical. They speak with a sense of revealed truth about nature, a religious-like faith that they know what is the TRUTH about an issue. They are righteous whether are not they are right. I find this sense of revealed truth about environment and nature scary. It suggests that there are some people with the real truth and others without it; that there are only two kinds of people -- the truly and completely good and the completely evil, nobody in-between, no blend of human qualities within a single person. It divides the world into environmental saints and sinners. It reduces truly complex problems about incredibly complex systems to simple answers.

That's what was so refreshing about Maggie's Bend, Whorehouse Jack and his employees and customers. Here were legally designated sinners confronted with the development of a legally designated wilderness. Parties on both sides sought a means to reach a fair agreement, and they did. To my knowledge, nobody had to stand up and admit who was and wasn't a sinner. In its own way, Maggie's Bend and the establishment of the wild and scenic region on the Clearwater River seems to represent the truly wild, the truly natural, as well as the truly human. It does so better than self-righteousness.

Such events, early in my career, led me to wonder what I was doing in the profession – the profession of ecology, that was supposed to be the study of the relationship between living things and their environment. What was I doing trying to apply this science to solve environmental problems in a way that was fair, objective, and good for people and nature? How had I gotten into all of this anyway? And was it a mistake, the right thing to have done, or was the universe just playing a big joke on me? I started to think about how all this happened. It began in three places: in a radioactive forest on Long Island, New York; in the Woods Hole Marine Biological Laboratory where I was working at a new "Ecosystem Center"' and in a nineteenth century water-powered mill in New Hampshire. Where had my career gone wrong? Or had it?

Nature is many things, but it is not self-righteous, and it isn't cast in black and white. There are not environmental good species and environmental evil ones. The wild is wild, make no mistake about it. It is messy, complicated, hard to hike through and hard to understand. It's dangerous and might kill you if you're not prepared and alert. Sometimes it's even fun. It's about as difficult to comprehend as somebody counting the towels in the laundry at a whorehouse in Koskoosia, Idaho.

CHAPTER 2

If You Use Folk Music, It Doesn't Matter What Color You Are. Everybody Is Welcome And It Brings People Together In Peace And Friendship.

I grew up with folk music. I made my first folk song record when I was six years old and have been singing and playing the guitar ever since. The most important thing I've learned about folk music is that in the past, during times of trouble, Americans used to always turn to folk music, including protest songs. But today, with all the various problems in America, with so much divisiveness, we seemed to have forgotten about the healing and health and joy that we, as an entire people, used to find in folk music as its way of bringing us together. In pondering about my main professional career as an environmental scientist, I began to think of another possible career path I might have chosen, and which had become a lifelong hobby and then a second career.

Many people I talk with these days, with the Corona Virus active, people being shot and killed on both sides of an issue, or because of their difference skin color --- say that what is happening today never happened before. They do not remember so much American history-- SARS, the great Flu of the 20th century, the Vietnam war, the Korean War, W W II, WW I, the Great Depression of the 1930s, about which Woody Guthrie (a famous folk singer of the middle of the twentieth century) wrote so many mournful and socially important songs, the civil war, the American Revolution. And few people know any history of civilizations before America, each of which, more than 100,000 years and more, rose up and then crashed down. And the causes of those rises and falls were often surprisingly similar to what led to the creation of the United States of America and what is happening to America today that may lead to its destruction.

During World War II, Woody Guthrie was a pacificist, but he joined the crew of ships carrying materials from the United States to Great Britain –- things Britain needed, from food to guns, to fight the war. He was a crew member on one of these ships, which were built quickly and did not have very much protective armory. He cheered his shipmates by singing and playing the guitar and making up songs about their life in these ships.

It was dangerous because German U-boats were out trying to sink these cargo ships. One night, the ship ahead of Woody's was blown up by a torpedo, and Woody wrote a song immediately that is still sung in memory of those times and of his life, *What were their names, did you have any friends on the good Roman James.*

TELL ME WHAT WERE THEIR NAMES, WHAT WERE THEIR NAMES?
(One of Woody Guthrie's well-known folk song)

Have you heard of a ship called the good Reuben James
Manned by hard fighting men both of honor and fame?
She flew the Stars and Stripes of the land of the free
But tonight she's in her grave at the bottom of the sea.

Tell me what were their names,
tell me what were their names,
Did you have any friends on the Good Reuben James?

Well, a hundred men went down in that dark watery grave
When that good ship went down only forty-four were saved.
'Twas the last day of October we saved the forty-four
From the cold ocean waters and the cold icy shore.

It was there in the dark of that uncertain night
That we watched for the U-boats and waited for a fight.
Then a whine and a rock and a great explosion roared
And they laid the Reuben James on that cold ocean floor.

Now tonight there are lights in our country so bright
In the farms and in the cities they're telling of the fight.
And now our mighty battleships will steam the bounding main
And remember the name of that good Reuben James.

Rather than stay at home in the United States and complain that nothing like this had ever happened before, Woody saw it as necessary that he participate, whatever the risk, and as a result wrote a song that helped Americans get through the War.

During America's history, in many of these difficult times, people turned to folk music, including protest songs, like *We Shall Not be Moved,* and it brought them together and helped them find peace and calmness. But today, when we have so many conflicts and dangers, few remember American folk music and the great benefit it used to provide to the people of our nation.

As I result, a music-video producer and excellent classical and jazz musician, Sergio Cavalieri, a Brazilian, and I got together and founded an LLC *called What Makes Us One.* The idea is to bring folk music back and have it played and sung —everywhere, at home, in Church, in groups of friends and family, across political divides that threaten our nation. Then once again folk music can bring back its role in healing and bringing our society back to peace.

We made our focus to find young people who were professional musicians but were unfamiliar with folk music. We would bring individuals and musical groups to Sergio's recording studio, and we would play them an old folk song ---- either I singing it, or we played them a recording from the past. Then we said, "Do it your way." The results have been great.

We have created a *What Makes Us One* "kit", including a DVD introducing folk music and folk songs, with some sung by old and new-comers; a 4" x 6" 50 page paperback book that also talks about folk music and its long role in human societies; and we two CDs of just folk songs.[1]

My family had been involved folk music and folklore from the early twentieth century to today. It began when my father, after growing up in Boston and getting an undergraduate degree, was offered a job in 1916 at the new University of Oklahoma (The university was founded in 1890.) He found himself at what seemed to be a different world. Instead of the big city of Boston, filled mostly with white New Englanders and a few other migrants include a small number of European Jews, he found himself in a small town surrounded for many miles by open grasslands, and the people living there were from a wide variety of backgrounds — Native Americans, whites from the eastern southern states, blacks from a number of southern states, and a very small number of people like himself, white and from New England. He was fascinated by suddenly living in so many cultures and backgrounds. He became especially fascinated with the folk stories and folk songs that came from each of these groups.

He loved all the different cultures and their different stories and songs. Didn't matter to him what background or color you were. He became an expert on American Folklore, spending his life at that activity and publishing many books. One of his books, *A Treasury of American Folklore*, was listed in 2012 by the Library of Congress as one of the 100 books that shaped America.

Eventually our family moved to Washington, D.C. in the 1940s, when my father became director of the Library of Congress's *Folklife Center*. Among his close friends that developed once we were settled in D.C. was a great American poet, Sterling Brown, a black man who was a professor at the university in Washington, D.C. He used to come visit us. He had a wonderful voice, deep and sonorous, something like the Dar Vader voice in the Spaceship movies. He wrote beautiful and moving poetry about the hatred of blacks by whites in the south, and with his beautiful voice he also told wonderful stories ---- some were very long jokes — and I would sit fascinated by him and how beautifully he spoke.

Brown was one of a number of friends my father made in Washington, D.C., some white, some black, some in between. I remember Sterling Brown because of his saying his poems and funny stories. He wrote of the terrible lives many black Americans lived in the America south. One of his poems was "They don't come by ones; they don't come by twos; they come by tens," about the southern whites who lynched blacks who said the wrong things or acted too independently.

I was told that one day my father and Sterling Brown were out walking in downtown Washington, and they came near the Capitol Building which housed the Folk Life Center. My father said casually to Sterling. "Why don't we go up into the Capitol? I don't think you've been there." Sterling agreed and the two walked up the broad steps and into the building. This seemed to my father and to me, a small child, just an ordinary thing to do with any friend. But my mother later told me that she was told that was the first time a white man had guided a black man up the Capitol steps. That may not have been true, but it was said, so it was seen by my family's friends and a good and important thing to have happened.

My father also became friends with a black man from the Island of Trinidad. I only knew him as Pappy, and he was very kind to me when I was just a small child at the time. Both of my grandfathers had died by that time, and so when Pappy came to our house and stayed overnight, he would take me up in his lap and I would sleep — he became my replacement granddaddy. I never knew that it mattered what color his skin was, and he didn't mind what mine was.

He would make occasional trips to Washington and my father would listen to, write down, or record Pappy's folk stories.

My father had many friends who were either folk singers or folk lore collectors (some were both), and they loved folk music from societies around the world. One, Alan Lomax, was a white Texas native. He and his father became fascinated with the wonderful folk songs black people in the south sang. Some of the best singers and guitar players of this music were black men in jail, one of whom was named

"Leadbelly," and he was a great musician. The Lomax father and son because so appreciative of Leadbelly's talent that they, as Texans, went to the then governor of the state where Leadbelly was in jail, and got him released, so I was told as a child. They then took Leadbelly to New York City where he became famous, a pop music idol known widely.

Alan and his father recorded or wrote down the music and words to many of the folk songs across the American south, some from white hillbillies, and some from blacks. Alan was also a guitarist and singer, and he learned many of those songs and recorded them. You can still find recordings of Leadbelly and of Alan Lomax singing, each on his own, some of these songs. Yes, color didn't matter; it was what you did and could do that was the difference.

Alan became a close friend of mine as I reach teenage years and for the rest of his life. He used to come to our home, then in Croton-on-Hudson, NY, sit on our worn out couch in the living room (he was a big man and the couch always sagged under him). He would talk to me about folk music because I too was fascinated with that music. (I made my first folk song record when I was six years old, recorded at the Library of Congress.)

One day Alan came in all excited, sat down and began talking. "Dan, I've been thinking about the difference between European and East and southern Africa native music. There are fundamental differences between them, differences that have lasted centuries — you know, the European music which includes opera, classical, and popular music. The singers in Europe, and therefore the whites who moved to the United States, always sang in tones higher than their speaking voice. And of course, there were all the other unique things about western

European music in the kinds of instruments, the way chords were used, and written down and so forth.

"Meanwhile, my father and I have been going to southern Africa and recording, listening to, and appreciating their music," Alan continued. "There are fundamental differences between their music and the Europeans. For one, the southern Africans sang within the vocal range of their speaking voice. And then of course there was all the use of drumming of a great many kinds, that did not exist in European music."

I knew he was right about that, because one time before he had brought some records that he and his father had made in Africa. There was one in which a single man sang a very nice melody and there was a wonderful rhythm that didn't sound like a drum, but was a brighter sound, more in the musical range this singer sang. Alan told me that that rhythm was made by the singer as he moved the top of a tin can against a rock. I thought it was great rhythm and still love it; about the best thing I've ever heard of to do with an old tin can lid.

"Dan, these major differences between southern African and European music has continued for centuries. I've been wondering for years how the kind of music could be different and persist over centuries in these two very different cultures. Very few things last centuries. On my way over here, the answer came to me ---- I don't know why I hadn't figured it out before. It was continued from one generation to another because mothers always sang to their infants as they nursed them, and that's why different musical styles have persisted for so many centuries."

It was fascinating to me, as it was to Alan, and I was flattered and pleased that I, still a teenager, was in Alan's eyes I was intelligent enough and familiar enough with folk music for him to share this new discovery with me.

Pete Seeger, probably the most famous folk singer of the twentieth and this century (until he died a few years ago) was also a family friend. He and his family lived not too far north of us in Beacon, NY. He too was deeply involved in folk music from many cultures. He and his wife traveled widely around the world, filming and recording music from many different cultures, many kinds of people. He then helped form a quartet called *The Weavers*, who recorded pop records, most based on folk music Pete had learned from his travels, or the Weavers singers knew from their childhood. Four of these records reached number one on the monthly popular music lists in the Rock and Roll age. Pete also, as a close friend of my father, would come down to Croton and he too became a lifelong friend of mine, a man I always greatly admired.

It wasn't just a small group of people whom you might think of as highly educated scholars and formally trained musicians. Not caring about what color a person was also happening with the Virginia folk music Carter Family, famous-to-become. At the start, there were three members who formed a folk song singing group: the husband, A.P. Carter, his wife Sarah (with a nice soprano voice), and her cousin, Maybelle Carter, who was a great guitar player, inventing the finger-picking style that lets the musician play the melody and harmony together on the guitar. It's the method I've always used and still do.

The Carter family began singing professionally on the then very new radio and making the then very new 78 rpm records. It is said that they were so popular that they had a lot to do with both records and AM radio programs becoming popular in many, many homes in America. A.P. was responsible for finding the songs and let the two ladies do most of the singing. At first, he just used all the folk tunes familiar to the family and their friends — singing together was one of the brightest and cheerfullest things people could do.

But then A.P. began to run out of songs, so he took to driving around the Virginia countryside seeking other traditional songs. Along the way, he got working with Lesley "Esley" Riddle, a black man who could play the blues and many traditional folk songs. The two worked together for years. Leslie was a much better musician that A.P. and he did most of the working out of chords.

A.P. and Lesley traveled together around Virginia. At that time, black people were not allowed to stay in hotels or eat in restaurants that were used by whites. A.P. and Leslie became great friends, and whenever they had to get a meal or stay overnight, A.P. would find Leslie a home that welcomed him and then A.P. would go to a restaurant and buy meals that he brought to Leslie. Once again, when it came to folk music, it didn't matter what color your skin was, as long as you could write lyrics, create harmonies, and sing.

I have carried on this tradition. My wife Diana and I were spending half the year in Florida, and I decided I had reached an age where I should make recordings of my singing folk songs and playing the guitar. But I add an additional thing. Having grown up the son of a folklorist and with such wonderful folk musicians and folklorists that became my friends, I knew the stories about the history and origin of the songs. So I introduced each song as I recorded it with its history.

I practiced hard until Diana, who is a wonderful musician, said it sounded good enough, and I went to a professional recording studio and started recording. I was thinking I was just creating these recordings as memories for my family. But I was very fortunate that day because the music-video producer who did all the recording was Sergio Cavalieri, a Brazilian. When I took a break, Sergio said "Dan, this is too good stuff to just leave behind. You've got to do more with it." He explained to me that he had been trained in classical music and loved Bach most of all, but also played in a Christian Rock and Roll band that sold huge numbers of albums, enough for him to be able to move to the U.S. He offered to play with me and teach me a lot about his music and his more jazz style of guitar playing.

We started talking about how we would approach this. Sometimes when we took a break in that first recording session, we would go into a nice waiting room where there were always other musicians waiting their turn or taking their breaks. This was, like today, a very difficult time in America, and it was very tense outside in the streets. But in this waiting room all was calm. I had a nice guitar and shared it around, and everybody loved it. There were people of all colors and backgrounds, but again that didn't matter. We were all just glad to be together, sharing about our love of music.

After one such break, I told Sergio about my growing up and about American folk music. I told him that in the past in America, when there were times of trouble, people always turned to folk music including protest songs, such as *We Shall Overcome*. But at the time we were talking, the only peaceful place I knew what this calm waiting room filled with musicians, all interested in each other's style and approach and chords and songs.

I said, "Sergio, today America is in one of those tough times, lots of anger, lot of bad things happening, but few people remember — know anything about----folk music.

We decided to set up an LLC, which we named "What Makes Us one," because that was what folk music did. We decided to focus on young professional musicians who had no knowledge of folk music. We would then play each of them a traditional folk song (sometimes playing an old timey record; sometimes me singing and playing the guitar) and said 'Now to it your way.'

The results were amazing, not just to us, but people who have listened to the results. For example, one young woman from Chile, trained to be an opera singer, came one day. I heard her sing and thought she had the perfect voice for an old Scottish song I had learned many years before while living in Edinburgh, Scotland. The song was *Died for Love*, a song that I had carried with me, often singing it as I went for walks, especially when I needed to cheer myself up. She recorded the song, and whenever I play her singing it, people in the audience invariably say "I could listen to her all day."

As a result of all of this, I say bring back folk music. It helped us deal with past terrible times and can help us again. And as I wrote down the other stories in this book and think about my career choice—to become an environmental scientist and keep folk music as a hobby most of my life — I sometimes wonder if I made the right choice.

The many stories about my life and career will give you a chance to decide which career I should have followed.

CHAPTER 3

How Many Hours Does A Whale Sleep?

**And other innocent but unanswered questions about
whales, at least when I needed to know them**

I got my doctorate in biology at Rutgers University in 1968 and was immediately asked to join the faculty of Yale University's School of Forestry and Environmental Studies, which I did. My thesis research had been a study of an intentionally made radioactive forest at Brookhaven National Laboratory. It was made radioactive as a test of what might happen to forests if there were a nuclear war, which was a serious concern in those day. Brookhaven Lab introduced me to the then high tech of many aspects of scientific research. Sometimes in my career, everything seemed to have gone right, but there were other times when things went very wrong. Usually, it was because the field researchers told me stories about what they were studying in wilderness, or of endangered species, which turned out not to be true. Here's one of the strangest and in retrospect funniest of this second kind of research project I did.

Whales, Whalers, and the Conservation of Marine Mammals

I was invited to a conference about the harvest of large whales. This had come about because the Japanese were among the nations that hunted large whales. The total number of whales that could be caught in a year was determined by an international conservation organization. At this meeting, the Japanese delegation proposed that there were too many large male sperm whales, and these were have detrimental effects of the population growth of whales. They said that the number of mature male whales allowed to be caught should be increased.

I was approached at the meeting, through a British mathematician I knew, named Charlie. He said that this organization would fund a mathematical and computer model study of sperm whale breeding behavior, to see whether the removal of some of the big males would make a difference in average reproductive. Here was the plan. We find out the details of whale social behavior.

We talked with open ocean whale experts, who told us what the lives and social interactions were of the great whales. From that information, we would create theoretical models of whale social and sexual behavior. Then we tried to find out if our computer forecast agreed with observations of the whales on the high seas.

I did this computer programming with Dr. Lilian Wu, a young woman who had just recently gotten her PhD in the mathematics field called game theory. She became fascinated about the forests and the wildlife, including elephants, that I was studying. And she was very good at a mathematics I knew little about but was the appropriate mathematical approach for this computer model of the social behavior of sperm whales.

Computer gaming simulation of something like the social behavior of whales may seem impossible and did so for most ecologists ---- my field — as well as some mathematicians not familiar with game theory. At that time, when computer models were new, to most mathematicians, these simulations seemed sham mathematics. To most biologists, computers were an unknown entity that seemed to have little to do with their work. I was one of the few ecologists at the time intrigued with the potential power of computers.

Several months later, Charley came back and we met with a whale scientist, Richard Needles, a Canadian. "Here's how sperm whales' social behavior works," he said. "There's a pod of whales---the females and their young. During the reproductive period, a pod has a single male, the harem master. He mates with the females. Some pods haven't any adult males."

"Then there're adjacent males, ones on the breeding grounds, but without their own pod," Needles said. "They swim round looking for a pod without a harem master. Or sometimes they try to displace a harem master. Then there are other males---immature teenagers and others who just give up on mating. They go up to the Arctic feeding areas." He asserted this was all true, and he bragged about how valuable his working on small ships on rough oceans his field research was.

Taking what he had told us, I had to find out how far these whales could hear one another and therefore communicate. I contacted an oceanographic Institution which housed one of the world's experts on whale sounds. "How far can sperm whales hear each other when they call?" I asked. "About fifty miles," he answered, but he looked at me quizzically. "Why do you want to know? I thought you studied elephants and trees." "It's a long story---sometime over a beer," I said, and hurried away, anxious to avoid another embarrassing conversation about who and how whales should be studied.

With that, I thought, I had enough information to create a computer game about the courting and sex life of sperm whales. Lilian and I worked out a computer game about sperm whales and whalers. Here's how the game worked. Imagine a chessboard, only with many more squares---let's say a board about three feet by three feet, with hundreds of squares. The game had two kinds of pieces. One kind was a largish oval shaped pieces called a "pod" that covers about six squares; it represented the group of females and their calves that Richard had told us about. The other piece, in the shape of a whale, was small enough to fit in one square; these were the male whales. The board had a small number of pod pieces---let's say twenty. (We spoke about this as a real board and pieces, but in reality this was all done as a computer model.)

You set up the game by throwing these on the board at random---say, equivalent to turning your back to the board and throwing the pieces over your shoulder onto it. Two players, one on each side of the board, had a pile of male whales. Now the game began. Each player takes one male at a time from his stack and puts it on the far right square in the first row. Then you and the other player each throw three dice. The left die determined how many squares the whale may move up the board, the middle determined how many squares it may move horizontally, and the right one determined if the horizontal movement is left or right-odd means go left, even means go right. This way, a male whale piece "moved" completely at random until it got within two squares of a pod. Then the odds change and there was a much greater chance of the whale moving toward the pod. The chances were set so that they increase again when a "whale" got one square away. That's because the male can "hear" the female and young whales in the pod.

You win a point by getting a male on the same square as a pod. Your whale can be displaced by one of your opponent's, if his whale lands on a pod where you already have a male. There is some kind of dice rolling here, too, to determine whose whale gets to stay. Whales that end up on your opponent's first row have "gone to the Arctic" and are out of the game. The winner is the player who had the most males on pods for the longest time by the end of the game. You get one point for each play that a male is on a pod. A point is a new calf. So you win by having the greatest count of calves.

That was the general idea of this computer model — the details differed in the computer game we created to more closely resemble the story about whale social behavior that Richard Needles had described to Charley. Lilian, and me. This would be a slow game to play by hand, but we wrote a computer program that created the board and the game and ran it very fast many times. We could play the computer version with various numbers of pods and males. Then we could make a graph of the average number of calves produced in relation to the number of males.

When we created this game, we had a computer simulation of a little bit of the whale's social behavior as told to us by whale scientists. Based on information we obtained from Richard Needles, we added courting and mating of the whales to the game and the chances that all of this would result in the birth of baby whales.

We spent several months to get this program to work. As far as we knew, nobody else had ever tried to make a computer game about the courting and mating of big whales, or even about any animal's social and sexual behavior, not even human behavior. We were very proud of our work.

After a few more months, the computer game seemed to work well. We began to get interesting results about how much the number of baby whales changed with changes in the number of mature sperm males, both harem masters and adjacent males---the ones the Japanese wanted to hunt. The results were different from any we had seen written about before, and we thought we had the chance to write an important paper with a new insight about animal reproductive behavior. Just over the horizon lay an ocean of success.

But then a question arose and our poor computer model got lost in the waves. How long did a male have to be harem master---to be with a pod-for successful reproduction? Were these overnight stands, just long enough to mate successfully with each of the females? Or were these long-term relationships? Did the male have to be there for the entire breeding season to protect the pod? And what happened if one male came in and forced another out-divorce whale style? I decided it was time to ask more questions of Richard Needles.

"Some good ships right here in Woods Hole," he said. "I should get you two out on 'em," he said. "Better yet, come to Canada. I'll show you what studying whales is really like. We'll go out in my boats. That's real science. Out in an open boat, watching the whales. Not the kind of garbage you guy do, sitting in an office scribbling on a pad, or even worse, using a newfangled computer. What's the world coming to, I'd like to know."

"We're making pretty good progress," I said. "We just have a few final questions." I cleared my throat and paused. "What happens if one harem master is chased out and replaced by another?" I asked. "Does the first harem master have to be there just long enough to mate with the females, or does he have to stay?"

"Oh," said Needles, "we can't tell one whale from another. We have no idea about that." I was startled. "If you can't tell one whale from another, then how do you know any of the story you told us about their social behavior is true?" I asked. There was a long silence. "Well," said Needles, "gazelles do it in Africa."

'That's it?" I said.

"Yes. We just assume that the whales behave like gazelles in Africa."

"You can't do that," I said. "We worked for almost a year to develop a computer model that mimics exactly what you told us. And now you're telling us you don't know if any of it is true. The whole thing's a god-damned fairy tale."

"Science is more than rolling about in your bloody open boat," I said. "Nonsense," said Needles. "We're out there where the action is. You guys sit inside and never see what you're studying. Now you're criticizing me because you don't like what I tell you I saw."

"You just told us you didn't see anything---you made it up because you think whales are gazelles."

Needles got up from the table, mumbled something to the effect that

people who use computers don't know anything about whales and stormed away. Our year of work on the computer model had just been hit by a tidal wave and sunk. The flotsam and jetsam of the programming was a beauty with no more basis in fact than the life of a unicorn. It gave fascinating results based on a totally mythical story told to us by a supposed expert on the behavior of whales. Except as an example of a hypothetical population, our work had no real application to the problem of hunting sperm whales.

Several years later I told this story to my old friend and professional colleague, Lee Talbot, one of the world's experts on conservation of nature. He had done some of the first fieldwork on big game animals in Africa years before. Lee laughed when I told him the story.

"I'm probably the culprit," Lee said. "I met with Richard Needles a while before he first talked with you, and I told him about the social behavior of gazelles I had studied in Africa. I told him about harems and harem masters, and how the male harem master defends his territory.

"He must have just transferred what I told him to believe it applied to whales."

It's hard to study whales. These huge animals are hard to find. Understanding has come a long way since that time. Ways have developed to recognize individual whales based on individual marks–cuts or markings on the tail, a certain shape to a jaw. Some whale biologists keep elaborate photographic notebooks, with entries about the sightings of individual whales. Today there I know some excellent experts on whales who use modern equipment including satellite tracking and field tracking. Perhaps today it would be possible to make a computer game that was accurate about how whales courted, kept their me pods, and managed they're young. But there are still the Richard Needles's of this kind of "science"–what I call the plausibility theory–if it sounds good it must be true. Informal observations substitute for careful measurements, the search for understanding, and the development of theories that are tested by observation.

I had become an active research scientist, still believing that I was part of a new but real science, a hard science, based on facts, solid scientific observation, and good theory. That theory was connected to observations, following the classic methods of science well.known in the physics. I still hoped that I could make a difference with that science, helping to apply it and really solve important environmental problems.

But then I began to come across strange problems---like how many hours does a whale sleep---questions so simple that you would think only a child would ask, but questions I needed to know the answer to, and could not find.

So, our wonderful computer game did not help save the whales and could not be used to increase our understanding of real whale behavior. In those days, nobody thought about software as something to sell; it was too arcane an activity to have much of a market, we thought. Perhaps today one of the computer game manufacturers could make an educational and entertaining whale mating game, a kind of animal pornography that might appeal to a certain audience.

Well, that was an example of early computer programming in the second half of the twentieth century. An important takeaway is that computer software was then and often is still condemned because the forecasting method is inherently no good. But in this example, there was nothing wrong with the computer program; it was the misunderstanding of what empirical science was by those focused only on that and misunderstanding it, and therefore a fundamental misunderstanding of what formal, including mathematically based, scientific theory was about nature in the twentieth century.

Fortunately, there is today much better research on whales. I was fortunate to be approached by Whale expert — historian, anthropologist, with a 60 foot steel-hulled sailing sloop capable of allowing him to study whales, their history, and the modern Eskimo whalers, who appreciated him so much that they made him a member of their open whaling boat. (See Chapter 17.)

I wish I could say that such misunderstandings of the fundamentals of the scientific method has gone away in the study of nature, ecosystems, life, and people. But unfortunately, these kinds of misunderstandings are still common, although perhaps not the rule, If you are curious about this some more, you might read another of my books, *Twenty-five Myths that are Destroying the Environment.*

CHAPTER 4

Repairing the Mill

During the time that I was working the irradiated forest at Brookhaven National Laboratory on Long Island, NY, and in the Marine Biological Laboratory at Woods Hole, MA, I spent vacations and weekends in rural Alstead, New Hampshire, helping my father-in-law, Heman Chase, a country surveyor, with his work and his hobbies. His main hobby was a working water-powered mill, the best of nineteenth century technology. Traveling back and forth from rural New Hampshire to the Brookhaven National Laboratory and the Marine Biological Laboratory at Woods Hole, both with large facilities full of modern scientific equipment, I was traveling from one century to another, and the experience was often jolting.

Heman believed in independence and in a small, self-sufficient community that used its natural resources well and depended as little as possible on trade outside. He and I shared a love of technology and of nature. He was a strong opponent of big government – the kind of government represented by Brookhaven National Laboratory and the various oceanography research institutions at Woods Hole, MA, and I doubt that he ever understood why I was working in there. How could I reconcile these two lives, I wondered?

"If you believe you should give a dollar to the government, then you have to believe that it will spend it better and more efficiently than you would or somebody you know would spend it," Heman said to me one day when we were surveying an old farm grown back to woods. We spent many days doing such work, surveying land that was passing from open fields to forests and from farm and pasture to the homes of retired executives or to vacation houses of the wealthy. We enjoyed the forests, wetlands, rocky slopes, and hills of New Hampshire and Vermont through this work. And as we worked, we discussed politics, philosophy, economics, and just about everything about people, society, and nature. Heman patiently taught me the names of the forest plants as we surveyed through the forests.

I came to the southeastern New Hampshire countryside at a time of transition. It was still possible to make a living as a dairy farmer with as few as fifty milking cows. A decade later that would end with the introduction of new sanitary regulations requiring that all milk be produced with electric milking machines, pumped directly into stainless steel tanks, and from these was offloaded into stainless steel tank trucks, never touched by human hands, never in danger of contact with the dirt and manure of the milk shed or the barn.

Southern New Hampshire was at the time little known – it was out of the way for the major summer tourists, who took the cable car up Mount Washington in the Presidential Range of the White Mountain National Forest to the north; out of the way of huge Lake Winapasocki in the north-central part of the state. Summer visitors to Alstead were mainly city relatives of year-round natives, or couples who had taken early retirement and chose to escape the urban pace of New York or Boston. Some found ways to enhance their incomes doing odd jobs.

The local people who had lived their whole lives in and near Alstead, NH, were known outside this remote region to be taciturn, but to have a special, dry sense of humor. Among themselves they socialized by speaking little but saying much. Walter Burroughs, Heman's brother-in-law, was typical. One cold winter morning in Alstead, New Hampshire, I woke early and decided to go out to get the mail. As I approached the row of mailboxes mounted about chest high on a six-foot length of a 4 inch x 4 inch board, the community mail center, I saw Walter Burroughs approaching from the Brick House where he lived. Walter Burroughs was a country gentleman. Lacking formal education, he had a graceful manner and an ability to put others at ease. He was in his eighties and well known to have been, and to be, a heavy drinker — what we would call an alcoholic. Walter was a quiet drunk, never bothering anybody as far as we could tell. "Good morning, Walter," I said, "How are you?" "I'm all right," replied Walter, "for a man of my age and habits."

In the middle of one winter Heman and I were down in the bottom level of the old water-powered mill, replacing the flume, the long pipe that carried water from the mill pond to the waterwheel, providing the power to drive the wheel. The old mill stood beside the stream and near to the road at the top of a rise. It had an unmortered foundation of three-foot high glaciated stones, on which were three stories of the mill fronted by weathered, unpainted vertical pine boards, one of the picturesque architectural styles of rural New England. A cold wind blew in through the cracks in this foundation. Water from the mill pond leaked down past us, cascading onto a layer of ice and skidding down the millrun out to the opening downstream in the foundation and into the main channel of the stream. Although called the basement of the mill, it was more a construction over a mill stream cut partway into a slope.

Near the upstream wall where the flume came out of a hole in the foundation, carrying water from the mill pond to the wheel when everything operated correctly, Heman Chase struggled to shove a length of corrugated coated iron piping about three feet in diameter into place, and then fashioned metal clamps around the length of pipe. Then Heman and I pushed and shoved the rest pf this long corrugated piping in place. It was exhausting work, and it always seemed colder inside the unheated building in the New Hampshire winter than outside.

I thought about the laws of physics that told me why this was so. Each of us radiated about as much energy as a 100-watt light bulb. When we were in a warm room, the walls radiated heat back. When we were in an unheated building, the cold walls absorbed that heat faster than we could generate it, faster than it would be lost outside in the sun when the wind was not blowing. Air is a pretty good insulator, and you're warmer outside in winter on a sunny day than inside the wet basement of an old stone-foundation mill. But that knowledge gave me little comfort as my hands felt frozen against the corrugated metal.

My feet were almost numb from the cold and my nose and cheeks felt iced. We had to stretch and turn our bodies in awkward positions to move the big pieces of metal, sometimes lying on cold rocks, sometimes encountering ice and water.

The water that flowed passed us as we worked leaked from the ten-foot high mill dam just outside the foundation. The dam created a small mill pond just upstream from the mill building. Beyond that, upstream, a paved road passed over the millpond. The mill pond was fed by water flowing from a body of water called "Warren's Pond" a few hundred feet away. In typical New England understatement, this "pond" was what elsewhere in the United States would be called a lake, extending three-quarters of a mile to the north and spreading out into several coves. The pond's small dam, about four feet high and ten feet long, the mill pond and its own small dam, and the mill building had been there for more than a century.

From Chase's mill, the stream descended a steep grade, twisting through a glaciated valley. Walking along the stream, you could find the foundations of six other mills that had once been powered by the same water, all within a quarter mile of the remaining mill. Here was one of the small power centers of nineteenth century New England, part of the industrial revolution within this most independent village of this independent state.

"How many times have you had to replace the flume?" I asked Heman.

"Let's see. My stepfather, Hartley, and I began to restore the mill in 1917 when I was a teenager and we put a new flume in then. Since then I think I've replaced it twice more. Don't expect I will need to do it again," Heman said. He was in his sixties and took digitalis each day for his heart condition, and ate a diet heavy in cream, ice cream, butter, and rich meats.

"Time for a break," Heman said after we finished installing one of the metal sections. We uncoiled ourselves from our awkward positions, backs and legs against the hillside of the mill basement, and half-crawled from the upstream end of the building toward the water wheel. The flume, when intact, flowed about 40 feet horizontally and then made a vertical turn so that water flowed down a pipe and into a turbine water wheel. This wheel, shaped like a fan and similar in design to the blades in a modern jet engine or, on a much larger scale, a modern water-powered generator, was a relatively new invention in the second half of the nineteenth century. Not as picturesque as the big wooden undershot or overshot wheels of earlier times, which turned slowly outside the mill, the turbine was much more efficient, capturing much more of the water's energy as it flowed downstream. All the water falling through the flume down ten feet made contact with all the turbine blades all the time, so that much more energy was extracted from the water than from a wooden overshot or undershot waterwheel seen in nostalgic landscape paintings.

Having crawled and walked away from the beginning of the flume, we went down a rickety wooden stairway to the level of the wheel and inspected its condition. The outer housing of the turbine blade was partially encased in ice, but the external metal seemed to be in good shape. The wheel was fastened to a vertical metal shaft, painted yellow, that transferred the rotating motion of the turbine to the floor above where Heman and I had been working. On that level, the shaft was attached to a large pulley, about three feet in diameter. When the flume was intact and carried water to the wheel, this pulley pulled on a leather belt, about eight inches wide, that spun a horizontally mounted pulley about 20 feet away. The second pulley was fixed to a long horizontal metal shaft that ran almost the entire length of the basement, perhaps thirty feet, and on which were four other pulleys. Each of these spun other leather belts that transferred power to yet another pulley at the base of another vertical shaft. Some belts were horizontal and moved the rotating power across the basement to other pulleys; other moving belts went up, through the ceiling and turned woodworking tools – a planer, a joiner, and a drill press.

When the mill wheel ran, everything spun, thumped and moved, and the entire building vibrated – all five floors of it, if you included the partially open basement: one floor for the water wheel, one for the belts and pulleys to transfer power, one for the machines and wood and metal working shop, and one above that served as living quarters, if you could keep warm enough in the winter from its one fireplace and plank board, uninsulated walls. You had a sense that you were in direct contact with energy and power. It was huge and a giant demonstration of some fundamental laws of physics and rules of engineering —-plain to see---so different from the hidden electronic machines in the radioactive forest, or for that matter the radiation itself – invisible and deadly, sterilizing. Here in the mill was the dust of two generations of users flung about into the air, reflecting and refracting the sunlight that fell through the windows, energy made suddenly visible.

We climbed back up the stairs from the turbine to the basement level and then up another flight of stairs to the level with the belts and pulleys and inspected these. "Best way to teach a child about physics," Heman said, "you can see the energy transferred from the water wheel to pulley, from pulley to metal shaft, and from a metal shaft to a machine." On weekends he ran a shop class for local children, introducing them to woodcraft and to the laws of physics through a thorough tour of the mill wheel and its belts and pulleys, as well as of several cutaway working models of mills, one of which ran from a tiny spray of water from an offshoot of the flume. It was a clear example of nineteenth century industry and energy production, entirely mechanical transfer of water power.

We drank some hot cocoa out of a thermos and ate a few cookies and then descended to the basement and resumed our work, getting a second section of the flume in place by the time the sunlight was fading.

Then we stopped for the day and went up the road to Heman and Edith's home for a cozy dinner by a warm wood fire.

The next morning, we were back at the mill. The wood and metal working shop on the ground floor had some electrically powered tools, many hand tools, and four machines powered by the water: a drill press, a joiner, a power saw, and a planer. The primary use for the water-power was to plane rough boards. The water-powered machines were also of nineteenth century manufacture and were well made, as was characteristic of that period in America. The planer took a rough board that would put splinters into your fingers if you handled it without gloves and spit out wood chips and a beautifully smooth surfaced board. It was a mechanical marvel, about four feet high, four feet wide and six feet long. Its blades were a series of rectangular chrome steel sections put together on a belt, like treads on a bulldozer. They spun so rapidly that they seemed a blur and made a very loud chattering roar when a board passed through them. It took some skill to use the planer. If you pushed up or down on the board as you tried to push it through, the blades would gouge the board and make it unusable. The noise was deafening. Using the planer was another way I felt in direct contact with energy and power, as the planer grabbed the board from me and pulled it with great force. Heman said that the turbine blade generated fourteen horsepower, and you could feel every one of those horses yanking the board away.

A small wood stove burned brightly in the shop, warming the main floor comfortably even on this harsh winter day. As I had done many times, I looked around the shop room of the mill. Every nook and cranny was crammed with hand tools of the nineteenth and the twentieth century, along with partially finished projects – a child's model airplane, a partially completed three-legged stool, a reproduction of an iron banded carriage wheel partially assembled – as well as jars of screws, nails, fasteners and strangely shaped, elegant brass objects whose functions were unknown to me. There were hand saws, chisels, clamps, drills, and many objects whose functions were also a mystery to me. A half dozen or so work benches filled the spaces between the big power tools, and the benches were crowded with projects in various stages of completion and with tools left near the work. In one corner hung an old banjo clock, an antique little noticed, but which was later assessed to be of great value. I suppose that many of the other objects stacked in odd corners here and there and covered with dust were equally valuable and would have been a joy to a museum of technology. But here they were just part of the old mill, and many of these objects had been there for fifty years.

The main shop had two doors, with both open, it was wide enough to admit an automobile if the interior was cleared out. Outside the doors was a small parking area on the uphill side of the building. Opposite the doors, windows on the wall of the shop looked over the mill stream. The front of the mill faced onto the road and the millpond, which could be just barely made out through dust-covered old window glass. To the rear, the shop led through a doorway to a back storeroom, a room with shelves piled helter-skelter with hardware of all kinds that I had been inspecting. I had spent many an hour sorting through these items which had fallen into lack of use more than two generations. There were familiar objects: brass screws of many sizes in small containers; drill bits. And there were many pieces of hardware deposited there from an old blacksmith's shop that had once stood upstream on the side of the outflow from the lake, but had been taken down when it threatened to fall down of its own accord. These objects, having to do with horseshoeing, the construction of horse drawn wagons, coaches, and sleighs, were not comprehensible to me. Most were covered with dust and I believed that few people had looked at some of these in half a century. Sometimes when I stood there, I imagined that Heman's stepfather, long dead, was watching over my shoulder, and I wondered if he would be pleased to see a stranger such as myself fascinated by what he had casually put aside one day and then forgot about, item by item. Sometimes standing in a dusty corner the feeling that he was watching me and was a presence became palpable and I had to leave. So, it is with dusty corners of old buildings filled with large pieces of a technology no longer quite understood. I wondered if someday the radiated forest at Brookhaven, then so modern and advanced, would be another such attic of devices and memories.

Repairing the mill brought me in direct contact with a way of life different as could be from the high-tech science at Brookhaven National Laboratory and Woods Hole's various large research laboratories. It was an industrious small New England village, almost self-sufficient except for the need to import certain raw materials, such as the metals to be worked on in the mill, or some complex tools made outside. Producing for trade some products from the series of mills that once filled this short stretch of the stream valley, as well as milk from local dairies and other agricultural product, and some timber cut from the local woods. Most of all, it brought me into contact with a now-vanished world-view, a world in which how things worked was plain to see, bigger than a bread box, explainable to a casual passerby without much time to think about it.

The mill was as near a place of certainty in one's ability to control nature's power and sustain the use of that power as any place or any system I had known. It was part of a past world in which a small village of similarly minded people could lead lives that seemed reliable, dependable, and determined by one's own actions. Even in the cold winter, with ice on the flume's water, the mill, lively with good conversation, hard work, and with a seeming certainty that we would obtain our goal, seemed as comfortable and reliable a world as I could imagine. Even the intense ambitions, which led one scientist to sometimes try to denigrate or destroy another, seemed to have no presence here. Heman loved his surroundings, the streams and the woods, he loved his work and loved the people of New England. His idea of nature was a place to live within and enjoy a source of resources that one husbanded carefully. Some researchers at Brookhaven's radiated forest enjoyed the woods, but it was more a thing external for one to study than a way to live within.

Heman was careful in his treatment of the mechanical equipment, but he took electrical equipment, that more modern kind of technology — and less visible — casually. The wiring in the mill was the old-fashioned kind, made of separated copper wires covered by cloth insulation and these, running in parallel like toy railroad tracks, were attached to a series of wooden laths. The pegs on the laths holding the wires made convenient places to hang things, and many of them had clothes hanging from them on metal hangers, with the hangers touching both electrical wires. If the old cloth insulation wore through, the result might be quite spectacular sparks and perhaps a fire in the wooden mill building.

Heman had a big power saw that he had made himself from an old washing machine motor, a wooden housing he had built, and various old pieces of hardware from the mill's shop. To turn it on and off you had to use a big knife switch, a kind you don't see today — a U-shaped copper bar about four inches wide, hinged at the open ends and with an insulated rubber handle on the bottom of the U. To turn the saw on, you had to grasp the switch handle, as wide as your hand, and push it down into a pair of copper clips. This completed the electrical circuit and brought electricity to the motor, which responded immediately with a loud whirr to spin the saw blade. Heman had mounted this switch on the right side of the saw, about knee height, so to turn on the saw you had to bend over the saw and its big exposed circular blade, take hold of the rubber handle, and push it upwards so that it fit into copper groves that connected to the wiring of the motor. From my point of view, turning on this saw carried a double risk – if I touched the copper bar instead of the insulated handle, I might get a mean shock, and leaning over the saw I might cut off my head or cut deeply into my chest if I slipped and fell forward onto the blade as it started.

After a few years I couldn't stand it anymore and I rewired the entire mill myself with then modern plastic enclosed wiring and put a fancy, sealed, heat-protected on/off switch in a convenient location in front of the power saw. Heman looked at the elegant switch and gave me a puzzled grin, as if to say, "nice of you to buy that Cadillac of a switch for this homemade saw, and I'll use it, but I really never needed it." The rest of us, Heman's wife Edith especially, were happy with the new safety switch. It seemed to me that Heman drew a blank with the new technology, not taking it seriously as dangerous, nor considering it something to be respected and made beautiful, in contrast to his re-spect of love of old machines.

After several colder days of work, Heman and I finished the instal-lation of the new flume, and the mill sprung back to life, vibrating, spitting out wood chips, spewing water through the turbine wheel. Reliable machinery of good iron, steel, and brass, carefully made, art-fully designed.

"This is the way everyone should live," Heman said to me as we watched the mill work once again. "Be independent. Nothing better than a country village life. Trade as little as possible with the rest of the world. Do what you want. Rely on yourself. Make and fix whatever you need." The Brookhaven radioactive forest with its complex and, for the time, miniaturized computer equipment, its mysterious silent radioactive source, its loud pumps and paper punch, its miles of electrical wires and plastic tubes, seem another world, another universe. And the same for the oceanographic facilities at Woods Hole. I seemed to be living in two centuries, the nineteenth and the late twentieth, each unexplainable to the other. I did not want to have to choose between them and believed that science and engineering could carry me through to enjoy them both indefinitely. Or I hoped they would.

Somehow, I had to put the two worlds together, the mill and the streams and forests in New Hampshire and the computers and radioactive forest on Long Island. I was trying to find my place in nature and in civilization, to understand how nature worked and how societies functioned. It seemed quite a different goal from admitting I was an environmental sinner and then getting environmental religion and righteousness, or from counting towels in Maggie's Bend. But the difficult, strange, poignant and funny incidents that this attempt would cause me were still in the future and did not occur to me at all as I helped Heman attach the final section of the flume to the turbine water wheel, our feet standing on frozen stream water in the midst of a New Hampshire winter, now so long ago and so far away in its view of the world.

As my life and career moved on, there were decades after Heman died that the mill just sat there, decaying. Many of us who spent time in Alstead wished someone would take it over and fix it up. And finally that happened. A younger group of city people began to move into Alstead, and some of the formed a small nonprofit corporation and began to get funding to restore the mill. They formed the *Mill Hollow Heritage Association*. If you look it up on the web, you will find the lovely statement: "*Since 1767 there has been a water-powered mill at the mouth of Lake Warren in Alstead, NH. Over the years these mills provided lumber for building, grain for food, and economic opportunity through manufacturing. Today, Chase's Mill is one of only nine such mills in the state. Under the stewardship of the Mill Hollow Heritage Association, a nonprofit, Chase's Mill will reopen in 2020. It will serve as a center for inspiration and imagination through hands-on learning for children and adults, through exhibits that look to the future as well as the past, and as a gathering place for the community.*"

People were invited to join this nonprofit and give money to restore the mill. Of course, I joined, and was able to attend the grand reopening of the heavily repaired and once again functioning Chase's Mill.

CHAPTER 5

Avoiding Deer In The Fog

One of the problems with trying to understand nature is that there is usually chance or some kind of randomness that affects what happens, so you cannot predict things exactly. It's like the weather —– the weather forecasters used to say things like "Rain tomorrow" or "Sunny all day," but now they rephrase their forecasts as the chance of rain or sunshine – "forty percent chance of rain." I soon became aware of this kind of limit to what we could know with precision about nature. Joe Pitalka, a friend of mine, worked for the New Jersey Department of Fish and Game and knew a lot about deer — their behavior, their food habitats, how to manage them. One day he was riding with Mike, a friend, in Mike's car along the coast of New Jersey near Atlantic City. They drove into a thick fog where they could see little in any direction. Suddenly, a deer dashed across the road in front of them, a quick ghostly movement barely missing the front grill.

"Better slow down," Joe said to Mike, "where there's one deer, there's usually others."

Mike slowed down. A few minutes later, a deer dashed out of the fog and ran into the side of the car, killing itself and doing severe damage to the door. If the car had not slowed down, the deer would have passed safely behind it. Joe understood deer well and his advice to Mike was based on that sound understanding. But understanding nature never leads to a perfect forecast. He was quite right about the group behavior of these animals. Deer often move in small groups and will cross a road together. But when the deer reach the edge, each hesitates a different length of time. Some are shy, some are bold. You can't predict exactly, from a speeding car, when each deer will cross a road. Ironically, if there was nobody in the car who understood deer, everything would have been all right.

Thus it is with nature and life in general. Sometimes no amount of knowledge is enough to make us completely safe or certain. There are always some risk, chance, and uncertainty, so that even the best forecasting methods can go astray.

In 50 years of studying nature and trying to understand it, I have found that, just like the deer running in small groups, we can make a reasonable forecast that a certain event will happen, but we are not very good at predicting when or where. Scientists call this the difference between a qualitative and a quantitative forecast.

Dangerous Nature in Beautiful Santa Barbara, California

This kind of uncertainty is a problem we have with all of nature and all of life. In the United States we seem to want to legislate and regulate such uncertainties out of existence. I became keenly aware of this when I moved to Santa Barbara, California to become a professor at the University of California campus there. Driving around, looking for a house to buy, I was surprised to see houses build on steep slopes, on slopes of soft soils that turned to moving mud in heavy rains, and next to dry stream channels, right down on the flood plain. We first rented a house in a pretty but narrow canyon just to the west of town in an upscale housing development --- the kind with a stone entrance with the name of the development in large letters at an entrance to winding roads. The creek bed, dry at the time I moved there in August, had eroded a two level stream channel, an upper flood plain where sediment eroded from the hills had been deposited fairly uniformly in the valley as the stream had meandered back and forth over the centuries. Then there was the present stream channel, cut below the larger flood plain where the stream now flowed. It was perhaps as wide as two houses. Anyone observant about natural history could see that the stream filled the entire channel during floods, and floods had to occur now and again, but there were some houses built right down next to the dry streambed, a disaster just waiting to happen.

And when such disasters happen, we seem to have come to assume that it is our right to live there and that somebody owes us payment for what we have lost, meaning of course, in most case, the federal and state government passing funds raised from citizens from all over to pay for the rebuilding costs for a few. We do not want to accept the risk and uncertainty about nature's climate. The real world of chance and uncertainty is hidden behind clouds of assumed certainty, and this leads to misunderstanding and misinformation.

When I did find a house I could afford, which we carefully chose to be above flood plains, and away from the worst wildfire dangers, I had to decide what kinds of homeowners' insurance to buy.

I asked Art Sylvester, a geology professor at the University of California in Santa Barbara, whose field of research was earthquakes, whether I should buy earthquake insurance.

"Well, I don't have it," he said. "The deductible's ten thousand dollars. If an earthquake did ten thousand dollars damage average to each house in town, it would bankrupt the insurance companies and the federal government would have to come in and bail everybody out, so in a sense, we're all insured anyway for free. The insurance premium is high, and the chances of the kind of earthquake that the insurance would cover are very low. Now, if I lived in a house that was mostly glass and did not have the kind of wooden framing that gives when the earth moves, or if I lived in a house on landfill, I might buy it," he added. "Of course, you've got to make your own decision." I decided not to buy earthquake insurance.

But I did buy insurance against wildfires, as did everybody else. Wildfires are common, the deductible was low, the premium was reasonable, and if you did not have wildfire insurance you would be out the value of the house, something I could not afford, nor could many people.

The choice of what kind of insurance to buy in each case, earthquake, and wildfire, was rational – based on an acceptance of the natural uncertainties and risks about nature. This is the way we need to deal with environmental problems in general.

When you are faced with discussions or decisions about nature, or for that matter life in general, remember the deer that crossed the road in the fog in New Jersey, and the man who knew about deer and did his best to avoid them in that New Jersey fog.

CHAPTER 6

Cigarettes and the Summit of
Mount Washington

Plain old human nature – competition between people, and the challenges between the sexes, also interfere in our abilities to get things straight and do the wisest thing. The power of such competition came home to me during a several day hike in the Presidential Range of the White Mountains of New Hampshire, a hike of professional botanists and ecologists who had agreed to take a relaxed pleasure trip through this beautiful country. These mountains have been famous, well known to Native Americans before the European Settlement of North America, and famous since then. Henry David Thoreau, the great nineteenth century expert on nature and author of a number of now classic books among the first to describe travel through Eastern American Wilderness and write about the character of nature, climbed these mountains and wrote beautifully about them. (You can read about his adventures and insights about these mountains in my book Botkin, D.B., 2012, ebook, *No Man's Garden: Thoreau and a New Vision for Civilization and Nature* (New York, Croton River Publishers). (Originally published in 2001 by Island Press, Washington, D.C., and still available from the author in hardback.)

This trip was an extension of a practice that Yale School of Forestry and Environmental Studies faculty member, Tom Siccama, and I had dreamed up when I was on the faculty at Yale University. Tired of being stuck in university offices and laboratories all day during much of the school year, we organized "forays into the environment," the silliest name we could think of for an excuse to get out and walk and look at the landscape and its life.

Mount Washington, the highest peak in the Northeast of the United States, gets some of the worst weather in the world. It is a curious mixture of the wild and, at the summit, the humanized. Near the summit there is a permanent weather station manned year round, the terminus of a cogwheel railway that takes tourists from the base to the top, a small restaurant-coffee shop connected with the railway, and not too far away one of the Appalachian Mountain Club Huts where hikers can stay out of the weather and obtain meals.

Mount Washington is famous as the location where the highest wind speed ever recorded on the ground in the Twentieth Century was observed. It was at the weather small collection of buildings at the railway station at the top of the mountain. It blew 232 miles an hour.

Three major weather system that travel across North America meet at Mount Washington: one that swings down from the Canadian arctic over the Midwest and the east; another that comes across from Washington-Oregon-Northern California; and a third that brings moisture up from the Gulf of Mexico. It has snowed on Mount Washington is every month, and the weather can turn quickly from a warm, T-shirt sunny day to hail and freezing rain and temperatures in the low 40's. Knowing this, we were prepared, but it wasn't a day to stroll along examining tiny flowers through hand lenses or gazing at the distant vistas.

I had often climbed these mountains, sometimes staying in hiking cabins, walking from one to another, for several days. Dealing with bad weather, however, happened to us on one of our group trips we organized through these mountains.

On the last day of this hike in the White Mountains, we found ourselves above timberline when the rain came so hard that it ran down our legs in sheets, filling our boots with water. It no longer mattered whether we walked in a stream or alongside it, our feet were equally wet either way, so I chose to walk in the stream where the going was easier, the rocks and pebbles formed into a smoother line by the moving water than the jumble of rocks alongside. We were in a saddle—that is a low passage shaped like the dip in a riding saddle---between Mount Washington and Mount Madison, above timberline in the Presidential Range of the White Mountains of New Hampshire.

It was mid-afternoon on the third day of our hike. Eight of us had started out on a lazy, humid summer afternoon at the foot of Mount Madison, some of us from Yale University and others from the University of Vermont. It was meant to be what we ecologists called a botanizing trip to explore the high elevations above timberline, enjoy the scenery, and try to identify and learn the plants of the mountains. But as was common on these mountains, the weather had turned bad.

We reached a decision point. The trail divided. One trail went up to the summit of Mount Washington, the other followed a stream in the middle of the saddle down to the road where our cars were parked. The eight of us stopped and talked about what to do, a discussion in the pouring rain. I had the feeling that if somebody were watching us from afar, they would think we were a little out of our minds to be standing in this pelting rain having a calm discussion about what to do next, the water pouring in sheets down our rain gear.

One of the eight was a young woman on the faculty at the University of Vermont who had been outdistancing everybody the entire trip, walking faster and longer and identifying plants quicker than anybody else. Some of the men took this as a macho challenge; she was not going to outdo them. I don't think anybody except this young woman was especially keen to make the ascent to the summit of Mount Washington, but there was a silence among the party as the rain poured down, the wind blew, and rolling clouds obscured the mountain peaks. The trail was well marked by cairns -- each a small pile of stones -- set about 100 feet apart. On the well-marked trails, built by volunteers of the Appalachian Mountain Club, some begun a century before, the rain was so heavy and the fog was so dense that we could just see one cairn ahead. There were cairns at frequent intervals, but the fog obscured the rest. It was wild weather in a wild landscape, however much people long ago had built beautiful paths within it.

My decision was simple. I had come to enjoy myself and learn about the alpine plants. This was not a day to do either. On previous trips, I'd been to the summit of Mount Washington many times. It wasn't fun in terrible weather, and I had nothing to proof to myself. I was going to take the path down.

But the other men waited to hear what the Vermont woman was going to do. There was a long and ominous silence. "I'm going up the mountain," she said, and started out into the fog on the trail that rose upward. The other men hesitated. If things got really bad, they rationalized to each other, they could take the cogwheel railway down from the summit.

Three of us, myself and two women, agreed that we would take the descending trail, get some of the cars and meet the others at the base of the railway where there was a parking area. Then we would drive the wet hikers back to their cars.

We parted and, as I waded down the streambed with the water soaking through my raingear, I thought about the five who had continued on up Mount Washington. I hoped they would be ok and imagined many kinds of disasters they might face. A gust of wind might blow one off a cliff. Soaked through, some of them might suffer hypothermia.

Our route down the mountain was hard enough. In spite of our raingear, we were completely soaked through when we descended to the elevation where trees grew -- about 4000 feet above sea level and a thousand feet below our parting with the rest of the group. I had hoped the trees would make travel a little drier, but I kept brushing up against limbs and twigs that spilled more water onto me than the rain had flung at me higher up.

Eventually, wet, tired, and hungry, we three reached the base of the mountain where our cars were parked. We changed into drier clothes and drove around the mountain to the base of the trail that our friends were to take down the mountain.

Near dark, our friends arrived. Tom, one of the five, and the most open and honest about his own failings and limitations, told me what had happened on the way up to the summit and back down. They reached the summit house of Mount Washington in midafternoon and went inside for a cup of coffee and snack and to make a decision about the descent. They were warmed by the little patch of civilization on the top of one of the wildest mountains in America.

The engineer of the cogwheel railway train sat nearby, drinking a steaming and inviting cup of coffee. They spoke with him about whether he had room and how much it would cost to take the cogwheel train down the mountain. He said he could take them, but they had to make up their minds quickly. "Last trip of the day," he said. They looked outside. The weather was getting worse, with the rain coming in sheets at a sharp angle to the ground, blown by high winds. Light was fading as the afternoon grew on.

None of the men dared say a word. None would be outdone by the woman from Vermont. Tom and the other men looked forlornly out the window. Bill, one of younger men spoke up. At first, he said he had decided to take the train, but hesitated when nobody else offered to join him. In the silence, he changed his mind. He would not be the only one to give in.

The Vermont woman said *she* was hiking down, whatever the others did. The rest watched the engineer go outside and climb into the cab of his train. They watched as the train disappeared down the mountain. Tom said the three other men looked forlorn, the woman looked resolute.

"The hike down was terrible," Tom said. "We took the Abel trail. It was very steep and water poured down the slopes like a waterfall. The wet ground was slippery and there were places it would have been easy to fall. We passed a plaque that we stopped to read, clearing our glasses so we could see in the dim light. It was in honor of somebody who had died while climbing that trail. A little creepy, given the weather," he said.

Finally, close to dusk, the party made it out and walked over to the lower train station. All the time, from the summit down, the Vermont woman led the way and the men struggled to keep up with her. None could.

When she reached the parking lot, she kept right on going past the parked cars in the rain to a kiosk, still going strong. The men followed, still not willing to let her get the best of them. She went over to a cigarette machine, opened her backpack, and took out some money and bought a pack of cigarettes. Then she opened the pack and struck a light and began to smoke.

"I thought all the other men were going to buy a pack of cigarettes as well, and start smoking, just to prove they were as tough as she was," Tom laughed, "And none of them were smokers either," he said with a chuckle.

What had started out as a pleasant, leisurely hike had, for them, become a gender challenge. They were wet, tired, and miserable, and they hadn't enjoyed themselves, but they had the pitiful satisfaction that they were not completely outdone by the Vermont woman. She kept ahead of them, but they had done everything she had done until they reached the cigarette machine. There, she finally outdid them. Even if they were smokers, they would probably have been too exhausted to light up. And if they smoked one cigarette, she would probably light up a second. She had beaten their spirit; she had won.

It seemed sad to me that the macho attitude -- or any hang up that forces one to do what he does not want to do out in nature -- had dominated the enjoyment of nature. It happened then and it happens now. Once out in a physical activity, some can't let go of competition when it surfaces. Yes. scientists who try to study the great outdoors are just people like the rest of us. Being a scientist doesn't raise us above any typical human failings. But this kind of intense, emotional competition can get in the way of finding out what is actually happening to nature and to ourselves.

I go to the woods to enjoy myself, to feel better, to be uplifted in spirit. When the weather turns and it looks like it's time to let discretion rule over valor, I remember the cigarette machine at the base of Mountain Washington and the young woman outlining and out-smoking some tired men. Of course I admired her; it was great in this time when women were generally assumed to be the weaker sex to see this woman prove she was tougher than the men. My sister, Dorothy, was strong, resilient, and a major high school academic prize-winner, so I had grown up with a sister as tough, or tougher, than myself. I reminded myself about the reason I go to the woods. To uplift my spirit and to learn a little more about nature. If I want to suffer, I can do that easily at home.

CHAPTER 7

The Monkey's Dilemma

Having chosen this profession of ecology and focusing on forests and their wildlife, I was always trying to figure out how to understand how nature worked — back to my high school need to know how everything works. Making forecasts about nature was hard at that time, and continues to be. One of the events that most impressed me about the limits to our forecasting ability about nature was a story told to me by Ben Sheldon when I was working on a forestry project in Costa Rica. Ben was the owner of a Wilderness tourist resort called *Paradisio Perdu*, which was in the wet and drizzly Costa Rican Rainforest. He had set up the resort as an ecotourism project, to introduce foreign tourists to tropical rain forests and to show that this way of conserving the rainforests could pay for itself, and be a private, rather than a public, governmental, method to help save nature.

Four of us working on a study of rain forests made the trip: Mike Marzolla, a friend who had come to Cost Rica as our translator and guide; Lloyd Simpson, a post- doctorate working for me in a study of the rainforests, and Lloyd's wife, Kathy. We had driven from San Jose, the Capitol City of Costa Rica, for several hours to a turn off where we parked at a small house and farm where a sign told us this was the starting point for the ride to Paradisio Perdu. A pretty little girl in a muddy dress stared at us from the door of the house. We and the other tourists then got into a long cart mounted on big wheels, with a canvas roof supported by wooden slats. This kind of cart was used to pull farm workers around Costa Rican banana plantations through mud and across rivers. A red, American-made four-wheel drive tractor with a crew of three Costa Ricans pulled the cart. The cart filled up with about a dozen people who were going to visit the private nature preserve.

Soon after we started off, the cart and tractor crossed two rivers – rocky-bottomed, clear-flowing rivers, lined on both sides by rainforest and farms. Water came almost up to the floorboards and the cart seemed at some points about to flow off into white water rapids that we could see just downstream. But the tractor huffed and pulled and got us across the rivers and into a muddy track that passed through cattle ranches, green fields, and scattered patches of intensely, brilliantly green rainforest trees.

The ride in the banana car took three hours over a very bad road of a heavily eroded red soil, almost a clay. At times, the tractor and cart got stuck among the mud and boulders, so we had to get out and walk while the crew pushed and pulled and manhandled the vehicles. The stops got more and more frequent, so we seemed to be walking as much as riding. It was a pleasant day and the walk would have been nice except that the clay-like mud of the track stuck to our shoes and made walking slippery.

We made a lunch stop part way up. There Ben met us, having walked down from his resort, and invited us to walk the rest of the way, rather than ride, and he would tell us about the rain forest. "It's only three kilometers, an easy hike," he said. This seemed a pleasant invitation and we agreed. He told us that the resort was relatively inaccessible on this terrible track because he wanted it that way, so that logging trucks could not use his roads to get in and begin to cut down the big trees of the rainforest.

Our walk soon became quite strange, with a tendency for some danger to us. Ben walked us through water that was halfway up our boots, making the heavy clay soil and rocks even slipperier. In places Ben had made a rough trail out of unfinished, half-cut boards that tipped on rocks beneath them. Any of us could have fallen and broken something, especially at the pace he kept up. Here was risk and uncertainty—one of nature's characteristics for human beings, I was learning-- foot first. As we walked, Ben told us about the local animals and plants. Now and again he stopped and stood in a drizzle under the trees. He was dressed in T-shirt and old gray trousers that had been re-sewn many times, and wore rubber boots. He talked rapidly and looked a little wild-eyed and intense, and by mistake he had zipped his fly so that the tail of blue T-shirt stuck out at the top of the fly, like an oxygen-starved penis.

He had been born in Brooklyn, Ben told us, but had lived in Costa Rica for more than 20 years. He was like other expatriates – American and European – that I have met in the tropics, especially on the outskirts of civilization – a sort of person you run into when you least expect it, although you get to learn that such people do live there. Like the deer crossing the road, you can feel certain that they are there, but you just don't know when they will turn up. They're like characters in a Joseph Conrad novel or the photographer who filmed the movie, famous at that time, *Apocalypse Now* who turns up in the midst of the Southeast Asian rainforest in the movie about the Vietnam War,– people who, for one reason or another, did not fit in at home and have left their native country to make themselves important in a developing nation, or to be able to act out their behaviors that they could not do in their home country. They are often interesting, but there is also something a little strange about them. They are another one of the surprises and bits of chance that you meet when you are out to try to study nature in a remote area.

Mike Marzolla, as I said our Spanish Speaking friend and guide on this trip, told me later that he noticed there were two trails that led from the tractor track and around to the residential part of the resort, and Ben had taken us on the longer one. He had not given us a choice, nor asked us how we felt, if we were tired, or hot. It took us about three hours to go three kilometers, or what he said was three kilometers.

When we had hiked for two hours I finally said to Ben. "Where is the lodge from here?" Ben pointed up the trail and he said "that way" which tipped me off immediately that he was really testing us. I never asked again, but he did offer at one point that it was about a kilometer farther on. He had gone out of his way to create additional uncertainty for us. Mike later referred to this as "the forced march." It was beginning to get toward twilight, but Ben had one more story to tell, which turned out to be worth the entire trip.

He took us off the trail a short distance to a small palm tree that, he told us, grew only in the understory beneath the tall trees of the forest. A large frond, perhaps three feet long, of the palm had been cut on both sides, sharply as if with a knife, from the edge to the large vein in the center, which had been left intact. The intact frond had a natural angle to it, and the cut made the outer end of the frond into a kind of little four-sided canopy. "Bats of a certain species make this cut," Ben said, "they like to build their nests under the frond, it's protected from the rain. They use the nests for only a few years and abandon it and make another somewhere else."

"Monkeys like to eat these bats," he continued. "But once the bats abandon a nest, forest wasps often come along and use the nest as a base to build their own."

The bats are fast, and if a monkey peers under the palm leaf to see if a bat is there, by the time he looks and grabs the bat is gone. But if a monkey grabs without looking, he might get a bat, he might get nothing, or he might get a handful of stinging wasps. This risk was inherent in the monkeys' life. There was no way to know exactly what was under any specific leaf of this palm, and there was no solution for the monkey who wanted to eat a bat but to take the risk or go away hungry. A monkey came to learn that some of the cut palm leaves did have bats and some had wasps – that much was certain. This was the monkey's dilemma – whether to grab under a leaf or not. It was just like my friend who was an expert on deer in New Jersey and I told about in a previous chapter, the one who knew that deer often went in small groups. As I told in that story, he used that good knowledge to warn us to be careful not to run over and kill deer, but his forecasts were no better than the monkeys seeking a bat to eat in Costa Rica. But in neither case could either the monkeys or the deer expert know exactly how any specific situation would turn out. It's a part of nature that makes it all the harder to understand and makes it impossible to make predictions with complete certainty. Chance is part of mother nature's kit of tools to make studying her difficult. It places limits on what we can know.

Meeting Ben Sheldon was a little bit like this too, because it seemed a roll of the dice when and if we would meet this kind of expatriate character on this trip to Costa Rica – I hadn't run across any others in that country on my previous trips – but, as I said, you can be pretty certain that his sort of character is somewhere in the outposts of civilization.

We had the opportunity to learn firsthand more about risk and uncertainty in a tropical rainforest resort the next day. We stayed overnight in a pleasant wooden building, octagonal shaped, where every room had a patio with a view of the nearby rainforest or down an open, grassy slope, to other mountains in the distance. Mike and I shared a room and enjoyed sitting outside, watching and listening to the beautiful tropical birds. The only obstacle to our view of the distance mountains was a large and ugly cabin directly between us and the vista that was the kitchen - dining area -shop and headquarters of Ben's resort. It seemed odd that Ben had chosen to place the work building directly in between the most beautiful view and the residential building, another kind of odd bit of expected event, a strange design by an expatriate hidden in the outposts of civilization.

The next morning, we breakfasted on the porch of the headquarters building, which was crudely put together and whose primary decoration was a large skin of a huge snake that Ben had hung on the wall. The porch was on the upslope side of the building, so the beautiful view of the mountains and forests was cut off from us. We ate, looking at the snakeskin.

After breakfast, most of the other visitors, led by Margorie, Ben's assistant manager, a British woman with a funny accent so it sounded Australian, went on a tour of the rainforest. Mike and I decided that we had learned a lot about Ben's forest from him yesterday, and we wanted to visit a famous waterfall on his property and to watch the birds, best seen in openings rather than within the rainforest.

After the others left on their hike, Mike and I walked down to the falls. The path went through wetlands where Ben had casually placed some loose boards that shifted under one's feet. It was easier than wading through the clay-like mud. At the stream side there was a crude path down a steep and muddy incline, where we almost slipped several times.

We found a small stream, maybe 20 feet wide, that flowed over a short falls and then over a very long beautiful falls, and we walked down below the second falls, admired it, took photographs, and talked with Ben for a while. Ben told us that visitors swam in the pools below the falls, but the water rushed quickly and looked dangerous to all but the best swimmers. Since most of the other visitors seemed unprepared in any way for a trip into a wilderness, we thought that a swim below the falls could pose a risk to that kind of visitor. The slippery paths also made us wonder how an average tourist without any standard hiking equipment might make out in this isolated place. We were soon to find out.

About 11 o'clock, Margorie returned from the hike alone – without the others -- and said very quickly that one of the visitors – a retired American schoolteacher— had fallen and broken her arm. The rest of the party eventually arrived, helping the lady with the broken arm. She laid down on the porch of the headquarters building, beneath the snakeskin, and she was clearly in considerable pain. There was not even the beautiful view of the rainforest and mountains to console her, only rough boards to lie on.

Ben had no splints of any kinds in preparation for this kind of accident. He had no stretcher, and almost no first aid equipment. He seemed totally unprepared for this or any contingency. Although he had told us a great story about natural risk and uncertainty, ironically, he seemed not to have learned the lesson his own story implied: be prepared for the unexpected. *Paradisio Perdu* had no pain killers, not even aspirin, and the schoolteacher was in great pain. We were surprised that this remote resort that presented many chances for accidents was so unprepared for them.

We asked Ben and Margorie whether they could call in a helicopter to evacuate the lady with the broken arm, because we dreaded having her ride out for more than three hours in the bumping banana cart. Mike overheard Marjorie say it would take 18 hours to get a helicopter and she didn't want that lady around for 18 hours.

Ben went off and got one of his workmen to cut some lengths of lumber he had lying around – 1 x 2's – to begin to make reinforcement for a kind of split. He came onto the dining porch carrying these cut 1 x 2's and a big piece of plastic foam and proceeded to whittle and slash at the wood. I thought that this seemed to be incredibly amateurish and dangerous. I decided that it was time to take some action to help the poor lady.

Lloyd, who was in charge of the field crews in my field research, had had more experience than I had in taking care of emergency situations, and his wife Kathy was trained in some kinds of first aid. I talked to Lloyd when he was packing his suitcase and suggested that he should come down and help out. Lloyd and Kathy came down immediately and did a magnificent job, taking over completely from Ben, rapidly making a good splint, and putting it on the woman's arm gently.

Flying her out by helicopter was rejected by Ben and his assistant, Margorie, who asked if the lady had the $2000 for a helicopter and saying there were only four in Costa Rica.Kathy, very distraught, asked if Ben had that insurance that would pay for a helicopter flight, and we were all shocked to begin to discover that there was no equipment, no preparation, no insurance, no plan for dealing with this kind of contingency in a place that was just an accident waiting to happen. It was a matter of risk, uncertainty, and chance, but it seemed quite certain that somebody sometime would hurt themselves at Paradisio Perdu.

To tell the truth, I thought about the Monkey's dilemma and that I and my companions had stumbled in an equivalent — either have a beautiful trip to the Costa Rican wilderness, or get hurt, like the Monkeys getting bitten when they tried to get a snack.

By the time lunch was over, Lloyd and Cathy had finished setting this lady's splint, and she was carefully walked down to the banana cart, with Lloyd, Kathy, and several of Ben's workmen holding her and guiding her as tears streamed down her face. Kathy and Lloyd and Mike suggested that perhaps she should be carried out in a kind of stretcher rather than driven in the cart. Mike, who was fluent in Spanish, spoke with the Costa Rican staff and they had offered to carry her out this way. And they added they would prefer to carry her all the way out because this would be much better for her than being bounced around in the bumpy car on the bad road. But Ben insisted that she go on the cart.

The Costa Rican driver of the cart went very slowly, because the bumps were so painful to the schoolteacher, and the driver seemed to be very kindly. We left *Paradisio Perdu* at 2:30 in the afternoon and reached the little village and parking place around 10 o'clock at night –

what had been a three hour plus ride up became a seven and a half hour ride down. All the time this lady was jostled by the cart and was in terrible pain. Lloyd sat next to her, supporting her continually. Mike sat next to Lloyd putting pressure on him so he did not get thrown around by the rough ride and could steady the lady. Kathy stood and bent over the seat and held onto the lady's hand to help support her arm. Kathy kept the schoolteacher's arm supported by a big foam cushion she had made up from material scavenged around the resort, and also supported the artificial splint. The lady was given a few grams of codeine that somebody had in their pack to ease her pain.

Kathy was furious with the amateurishness of the handling and lack of preparation and the general mediocrity and poor condition of *Paradisio Perdu* as of course were the rest of us.

The woman's companion, a nice person from Dallas, came to the resort only in shorts and a very thin tank top. As we rode down it began to rain and the water blew onto us under the canopy. The lady with the broken arm began to look poorly. She reminded me of the people who get hypothermia in the cold mountains. I asked her if she was warm enough as we came down through the mist and the rain, and she said something quietly to the effect of "not really" so I lent her my sweater, something I always carried in a backpack in back country, no matter what the climate, just for this kind of contingency. Marjorie walked behind the cart, having left the resort without so much as an umbrella. In the drizzle, she ended up borrowing my umbrella, and remained unhelpful and outspokenly unsympathetic the entire way down.

We crossed the river in the dark, once again with the sensation that we would be swept away into the rapids that we could only hear, not see, in the dark. Finally, we reached the parking lot.

A radio phone call had requested an ambulance, and it was there waiting for us at the end of the trail and took the injured woman to a hospital. We learned the next day that she was ok and had been well cared for at the hospital in the capitol city. I wondered what might have happened to her but for the knowledge and kindness of Lloyd and Cathy. Chance had caught up with her, just as it did with the monkeys who grabbed under a palm leaf and came up with a handful of stinging wasps. She had learned firsthand, but in a very hard way, about risk and uncertainty out in nature, especially in the kind of resorts built on a small budget and not much experience in the wilds.

A few years later we read in a newspaper that two German tourists had drowned at *Paradisio Perdu* while trying to swim below the falls that Mike and I had visited. It seemed that not much had changed at the resort. Thus, our visit *to Paradisio Perdu* confronted us in several ways with the uncertainty, risk, and chance typical of nature and of people's works within wilderness.

We often think that we can solve problems completely with total foreknowledge or go on vacation into the wilderness with little preparation, and that somebody will always bail us out of danger or, if not, the government is obliged to and will. Sometimes we are lucky and all goes well. Sometimes, you can break your arm as did this nice lady at *Paradisio Perdu*. Sometimes even when you do this you can be lucky once again and there will be people like Kathy and Lloyd nearby to help. Sometimes you will be stuck entirely on your own.

When it comes to conserving nature, we often think we can solve problems with the complete safety and exactness in just this way. But the monkey's dilemma and our travel to *Paradisio Perdu* always serves as a reminder to me that this is not true. We live in a world of chance, and in that world, no solution can be perfect, no forecast can be made without some chance of error, no trip to visit wild nature can be completely safe. We can estimate the probability of error in most cases. We can prepare for such contingencies in ways that were a matter of course for our field crews but were not typical of the average tourist to Costa Rica, who read about a wonderful experience to see a tropical rain forest at *Paradisio Perdu*, as several tourist guides described it, making it sound perfectly and completely safe.

In every environmental problem we try to solve, we can never know exactly when and if we will grab a solution or whether we will get badly stung. There is a limit to what we could know and predict at *Paradisio Perdu*, including the personality of our host, the dangers of his resort, and the story of the monkey's dilemma. It was another sobering conclusion forced on me about the limits as to how well we could ever understand nature.

Of course, much has changed in ecological/environmental research. We have so much more useful technology including communication. We ecologists do a better and generally safer job in our wilderness research. But there is always an inherent risk. Sometimes that risk is itself exciting and appealing, as one might compare it to the thrill of downhill skiing. I have enjoyed that kind of risk, but only when I go into it knowing what I will be facing and prepared.

CHAPTER 8

Trimming Elm Trees

Tim Wood and Hedley Bond were short of money. They were students at the Yale School of Forestry, and their courses had convinced them that they knew enough about this subject to act as professionals. They went into the business of tree-trimming. They were vigorous, outdoor young men, hardworking, earnest, and with good senses of humor. Tim was about six feet tall, with black hair and a thick black beard and pleasing manner. Hedley was a wiry Australian, about 5' 10", with a narrow face and a determined manner.

Their first job was to trim a big elm tree near the curb on a busy New Haven Street. The tree belonged to the owners of a gracious, white-clapboarded home, a classic New England house, except that the front of the house was dominated by an ostentatious porch with Greek-style columns holding up the overhanging roof.

Tim and Hedley arrived with a few saws and axes and some long ropes. The American elm was distinctively graceful and was once the dominant street tree in many towns and cities. However, a disease that killed American elms, was first reported in the United States in 1928. There were estimated to be 77 million elms in North America in 1930, but more than three-quarters of these were lost by the 1990s. Fewer

American elms remain today and their graceful shape is now unfamiliar. The disease is caused by fungus, spread by a bark beetle.

The American elm had a complex shape, the main trunk split 20 or 30 feet above the ground into two to four arching limbs that spread out in what people referred to as a vase-like shape. The result was a beautiful tree whose leaves, hanging down from the high arched limbs, shaded the street below without limbs and branches sticking out into the traffic. These limbs were thick and strong, usually more than a foot in diameter. Elm wood is extremely tough, in part because the grain spirals upward, making the trees difficult to split with an ax and wedge and difficult to cut when the wood is green. But the tree's intricate shape made it especially difficult to trim.

Tim and Hedley's elm was probably beginning to suffer from Dutch elm disease. One of the limbs hanging out over the street was dying. It was this limb that posed a hazard and the homeowner had asked Tim and Hedley to cut. They started in earnest, one of them climbing up the tree and the other putting ropes on the limb. They were trying to keep the limb from falling onto the street — possibly onto a passing car. Their plan was to tie the rope near to the end of the limb, loop the rope around the trunk of the tree, using the loop as a break. One of them would hold onto the end of the rope, pulling it against the loop. Friction would stop the limb from falling. Then they could ease the limb over to the lawn.

The limb was much heavier and stronger than they had guessed. As Tim sawed through the base on the limb, Hedley held on to the end of the rope, standing near the porch to keep as far from the limb as he could. When the limb began to bend, Hedley realized that the loop they had made around the tree trunk was not enough to hold back the weight. The rope began to pull him to the tree. Holding onto the rope, he rushed up on the porch and looped the end of the rope around one of the porch columns, expecting this to be made of solid wood and capable of holding the weight of the limb. But the column was a hollow facade. As Hedley pulled on the end of the rope, now twisted around the column, the column groaned and started to rise into the air, the weight of the elm limb pulling it out of its base. Hedley rushed closer to the column. He pulled with all his might, but the limb was stronger than he was and weighed a lot more. In a moment, Tim, watching from the tree, saw the column and Hedley pulled up into the air, neither one grounded. Only the overhanging roof was preventing the limb from crashing into the street and yanking the column and Hedley in a flying arch toward the street. Tim wasn't sure what to do first. If the limb fell, it was in danger of damaging a passing or parked car, possibly causing serious injury to passengers. The rope was threatening to destroy the column and possibly the entire porch, and perhaps injure Hedley.

A crowd gathered to watch Hedley's acrobatics with wonder and amusement. For a few more moments, Hedley and the column swung like pendulums, suspended from the air by a rope. Tim climbed down from the tree, joined Hedley to help pull on the rope. Their combined weight was just enough to bring the column back down to the ground and keep the limb in the air. But what to do next? If Tim let go, Hedley would spring back into the air. But Tim couldn't stay on the porch forever.

Eventually, a few men in the crowd joined in to help. One took Tim's place holding the rope and the other helped Tim finish cutting through the limb. As the crowd cheered, Tim pushed the cut limb, still suspended by the rope, over to the lawn. Hedley and the helpful stranger slowly eased off the rope, lowering the limb to the lawn.

So ended Tim and Hedley's career as tree experts. It was a lesson in homilies: the limits of academic education; the danger of a little knowledge; the limits of the enthusiasm of youth; the value of experience. When we seek to find practical solutions to the conservation of our forests, and when we do this from a distance, with little learning and less experience, we should remember Tim and Hedley trimming the elm tree in New Haven. It's not a bad thing to think about in confronting life in general.

CHAPTER 9

Weird

THE FOREST AT THE COMPUTER CENTER

Preconceived notions often interfere with our perception and understanding of nature and doing something successful about it. I have run into problems of preconceived notions in many situations. In the 1970s, IBM sponsored the use of then relatively new computers to do research that had benefits to American society.

Later in this series of tales I will write about how many leaves are on a tree, and why I wanted to know. As part of that quest, I was involved in a television advertisement by IBM that was about my research, done in cooperation with two excellent IBM scientists, James Wallis and James Janak. Most of the filming – four days – took place at the Hubbard Brook Experimental Forest in the Presidential Range of New Hampshire – the same National Forest where the botanists and ecologists chased after the cigarette smoking woman professor, but could not keep up with her. The major experiment at Hubbard Brook was clear cutting an entire watershed – about 100 acres – and comparing the effects on water quality and total runoff with an uncut watershed nearby. (A watershed is an area where any drop of rain that falls flows out through the same stream.)

IBM wanted the advertisement to be completely accurate in content and in personnel – anybody who appeared in the film had to actually work on the project, and the content had to be completely accurate to the work. During the four days we spent in the forests of Hubbard Brook, a professional film crew filmed everything – showers, changes in the lighting of the forest as the day passed, every piece of field equipment in use by one of the researchers, including graduate students, a person's hand moving over a topographic map of the forest – the director told me that it was much cheaper to film everything anyone could think of than to discover afterwards that something crucial had been missed, and the entire crew would have to return to New Hampshire. They shot seven thousand feet of film for an advertisement that used 270 feet, he told me, and this was a long ad – it ran, in its initial version, for almost three minutes.

Despite all of his care, the director decided later that he had not filmed everything. We had one day more of shooting which was to be done at the IBM Thomas J. Watson Research Center in Westchester County, north of New York City. We were supposed to spend the day filming our work with computers, but a few days before I went over there, they called me and asked if I could bring my hiking clothes and ecology field equipment, so we could film some more material with me talking about the forests.

About three in the afternoon on the day we had been filming inside the research facility, I changed into my field clothes – hiking boots, broad rimmed field hat, blue long sleeved, many pocketed field shirt and tan trousers. I put my large aluminum frame backpack on and walked out into the large and pleasantly planted landscaping around the research center. The research center had been built on an old farm and there were many acres of open land. This made a pleasant environment in which people worked on all kinds of exotic science that involved some kind of computing. The landscaping had been nicely done, and a long grassy path led from the research center to the main road. The path was lined on each side with trees, and the film director decided that if he put the film crew outside one line of trees, and if I stood on the grassy path with the other line of trees behind me, the scene would appear as if it were in the forest. In this way he could avoid paying for the entire film crew and myself going back to New Hampshire.

So an entire film crew set up their equipment a few feet beyond one row of trees – there was a cameraman, his helper, a sound man and his helper, the director and a producer, a few extraneous assistants and onlookers, and all their equipment. There was enough equipment to install a telephone line, highly visible from the path.

The director had me stand in the path in my hiking gear, backpack and all, face the camera, and talk about our research. This required quite a number of takes, as I am no actor. In the middle of all this filming, a man walked out the door of the research center and headed down the path. We were sure he would see the film crew and stop or go some other direction, so we just kept filming and I kept talking. But he did not stop. In fact, he walked quickly through the scene while I continued to talk, and the camera kept rolling. He looked straight ahead and walked right past all of us, seeming to not notice anything that was going it. That was one take we had to do over.

This was so weird that I mentioned it a few days later to one of the IBM scientists I was cooperating with, Lilian Wu, whom I mentioned before. A few days afterwards she called me to tell me a curious thing had happened. She said she had just eaten lunch with another member of the research center's mathematics department, and he had told her about the strange person he had seen on the IBM grounds a few days before. He said there was this man wearing a backpack and hiking clothes, standing on the footpath right on IBM grounds, and looking at the trees and talking very loudly too himself. "I walked by him as quickly as I could, I'll tell you," he said to Lilian. He had seen me standing in the path from afar, and the sight of someone dressed as I was and talking loudly led him to assume things about me that made him miss completely seeing the film crew and all of its equipment, even though they were completely visible from the path and their equipment was not completely quiet. I remembered this story because I realized that sometimes scientists behaved like this mathematician walking on the path, not only in their personal reactions, but in the way they observed and thought they understood nature when they were doing their own work. Their preconceived notions determined their conclusions.

I was reminded of the IBM filming experience years later when I made a trip to British Columbia and was taken out to see some modern forestry practices. The night before several Canadian foresters met me for dinner. The dinner conservation turned to odd behavior, and one of the Canadian foresters said that the strangest story he knew along these lines happened to a friend of his who was a rancher in the dry eastern part of British Columbia. This friend would make occasional business trips to Vancouver. Once he flew to Vancouver and forgot to take any raingear. He arrived downtown with only his cowboy clothes – a big Stetson hat, blue jeans, boots, the whole works. He was walking after dark in what he considered a bad part of the city when it began to rain hard. All he could do was pull his Stetson down tight on his head and keep walking. Up ahead he saw a lighted corner where, under an awning of a corner store, stood a group of punkers with Mohawk haircuts, purple-dyed hair, tattoos, cut-off tee shirts – typical dress, he thought, of some of the tougher and more dangerous city gangs. He was immediately wary.

Used to dealing with dangerous animals on his ranch, the rancher knew how to approach potentially threatening wildlife: Walk calmly, try to show no fear, and look no predator in the eye. He took a deep breath and proceeded on as slowly and calmly as he could, head down, not staring anyone in the face but keeping a careful watch out the corners of his eyes. As he passed the punkers, he said "Nice evening" – part of his attempt to demonstrate that he was not afraid, although he was. Nobody answered him. But as soon as he had passed the group, he heard one of the punkers speak to another. "Weird, Eh?"

Each side had its preconceived notions about the other. The rancher assumed the punkers were dangerous, and the punkers believed that anybody walking down a street in Vancouver dressed as a cowboy, hat pulled tight over his head, and without an umbrella or raincoat, was at least a little crazy. So, it is with much of our perceptions, even affecting how we perceive and deal with our environment.

CHAPTER 10

How Many Leaves Are On A Tree?

Parsimonious. That word went through my head as I looked around Jim Janak's office. There was nothing on his desk except a telephone. Not a single sheet of paper was visible. Nothing decorated the gray walls. It was an inside office with no windows. The metal desk was the same gray color as the walls, lit by a fluorescent light in the ceiling. Jim Janak sat at his desk, which was completely clear of anything except a single pad of lined paper on which he wrote with a black ballpoint pen. Jim was a theoretical physicist at the IBM Thomas J. Watson Laboratory, where I had come to spend the summer, at IBM's invitation, to work on what the corporation was calling a socially relevant problem. The federal government was suing IBM for bundling software and hardware, an anti-trust suit, and as far as I could tell, IBM had created a summer program for socially relevant uses of computers as a way to improve its public image. One of the topics the corporation had chosen was environment, and word had come to Yale University asking if there were anyone involved with environment who could think of a use for computers. I had been talking about my ideas for the development of a computer program that could mimic the growth of trees, and IBM invited me down for the summer. I had met with several IBM scientists and mathematicians, and two of them, Jim Janak and Jim Wallis, were interested in the ideas I suggested for a computer program that grew trees in a forest. We were soon immersed in the project, but this was the first time I had been in Janak's office.

I had never seen a scientist's office like this. Parsimonious was the best word I could think of. Entirely different from my own office at Yale with papers scattered everywhere, much like my office had been at Woods Hole's Marine Biological Laboratory. A universe of difference from the office of my Yale colleague, Tom Siccama, who had climbed Mount Washington and followed the woman botanist all the way to the cigarette machine. Tom collected everything and threw nothing away. Tom's office had a floor full of boxes of computer cards, bundles of books, piles of papers, published and unpublished, and stacks of unboxed computer cards.

Tom was a rockhound – a person whose hobby was studying geology out in the field and collecting rocks. Whenever he went on a hike, he carried a geologist's hammer, a small, narrow hammer especially made to chip samples from rocks.

Tom's collection of rocks occupied several shelves meant for books on one wall in his office. The shelves were the kind that were attached to metal strips on the wall which were in turn screwed into wall studs. The shelves were attached with tiny hooks to holes in the metal brackets. His shelves were twelve inches deep. I often admired Tom's rocks, fascinating and different one from another: a gray hard rock with small rectangular crystal-like shapes imbedded in it; a granite boulder from the Presidential range with a large band of white quartzite running through it; yellow sandstone with horizontal bands; a conglomerate with pebbles the size of golf balls sticking out of its surface. Some were large – about a foot in diameter – and heavy.

To get to Tom's desk or to his collection of rocks, you had to weave your way through the piles of books, papers and computer cards on the floor, through pathways that Tom kept just barely clear. When you came in to visit, he would graciously remove whatever he had piled on a wooden office chair set out for guests, and motion you to it. There you and Tom sat, surrounded by as much of nature as he could squeeze into his office along with much that had been written about nature. A great naturalist and expert on forests, Tom had told me with his wry sense of humor about the cigarette chase on Mount Washington, when he chose to follow the lady botanist to the top of Mount Washington.

One day Tom's collection of rocks got too heavy for the shelves and the shelves gave way. Rocks were strewn across Tom's office, helter-skelter, with little rocklets that broke off as they fell to the floor and the pieces scattered widely. I went by his office that day and looked in at the semi-chaos. The shelves were hanging precariously, some fallen to the floor, but Tom sat calmly at his desk working away, among the litter of rocks and papers. I was sure the shelves would soon be repaired, and the rocks reinstated in their rightful position on the shelves. But a month later only the shelves were fixed; Tom never bothered to move the rocks. Over the next months, I peaked in his office now and again and everything was as it had been on the day of the rockslide, rocks still laying where they had fallen, boxes of computer cards still on the floor, a new path created around the rocks to Tom's desk, and Tom was sitting there calming talking on the phone. As far as I can remember, the rocks were still on the floor when I left Yale and went to work at the Cape Cod Marine Biological Laboratory.

Tom's Yale office was in my mind as I stood in Jim Janak's office, in shock.

"How do you keep your office so neat?" I asked.

"Only keep the most recent copy of anything," said Jim in his usual compact and terse way, his speech as parsimonious as his office. When he stepped out of the room briefly, I couldn't resist. I opened his desk drawers and his cabinets, sure there would be a hidden stash of messy papers. Nothing. Not even a neat stack of papers. The office was empty.

Non sunt multiplicanda entia praeter necessitatem, William of Occam had written in the 14th century. "Entities are not to be multiplied beyond necessity." The phrase had become famous in modern science as "Occam's Razor," one of the fundamental principles of the scientific method. Translated into science, it means always choose the simplest explanation consistent with observations. It is the aesthetic scientific principle. Truth and beauty lie in simplicity. I knew the idea well, but I had never seen it manifested in a person's life. Jim Janak certainly followed this principle in his lifestyle. His office was the essence of *Non sunt multiplicanda entia praeter necessitatem.*

So was everything else about Jim. He engaged in no small talk. I felt we were friendly, and we certainly worked well together, but occasionally he and I would eat lunch alone at the IBM cafeteria, surrounded by tables of other scientists chatting away loudly, joking, laughing, teasing. Jim and I ate mostly in silence. Jim never filled any gaps of the silence during our lunch with small talk. No "How's your family?" Or "nice day isn't it?" We would eat in silence unless Jim had something of value to say.

Sometimes the silence would bother me. I wanted to be friends with Jim, so I would say something just to be friendly. But if it were small talk, Jim wouldn't answer.

Jim also never made a mistake. His work was always perfect, excellent, nothing wasted. He, Wallis, and I embarked on the development of the computer model of a forest, and it was working well. Each of us wrote part of the computer programming code. Computers were primitive by modern standards, and at the beginning of our work our link with the computer was an IBM Selectric typewriter. The computer would print out one line of the computer program at a time, unless you could specify a set of lines by their line numbers. This meant that you had to have in your head the structure of the entire program and, in detail, each line. Since there were hundreds of lines of computer code in the program, remembering all the locations was quite a mental feat.

The weaker-minded could get the entire program printed out and refer to it, but we were in a process of rapid development, and those printouts were out of date too fast.

I would have to think for a while and remember just where a line of code was and then try to type its revision. I could touch type, but still I made typing mistakes and mistakes in logic. Often, I had to refer to the printout of the latest version.

Jim never made any mistakes, and never looked at the printed program. He would know exactly what line of code he needed to fix, have the computer type it on the Selectric, and then fix it. Well, I exaggerate. By careful monitoring Jim at work, during the summer I did catch him making one typing error. And I think I remember once his making a mistake in his arithmetic or in his logic. Maybe. Or maybe I just imagined it – wishful thinking. *Non sunt multiplicanda entia praeter necessitatem.* That was Jim.

He was a kindly and gentle person. His hobby, I discovered about halfway through the summer work (hobbies were small talk, apparently, and not mentioned at lunch unless you knew and brought the subject up) was handcrafting wooden children toys – the wonderful old-fashioned kind – wooden cars with wooden wheels that turned: wooden trucks, tractors, automobiles. On weekends, Jim sold them at charity fairs. I forget how this information came out. I think one day one of the toys appeared on Jim's desk, in transit to a fair, and I asked about it. Jim never mentioned it again unless I asked him. Like his work with computer code, one parsimonious exchange about his hobby communicated all that he thought necessary. It was inefficient to repeat things.

Non sunt multiplicanda entia praeter necessitatem. This was fundamental to the work we did. We put nothing in our computer program that we hoped would grow forests that was not necessary. And we proceeded as William of Occam had advised. Step by step. Try the simplest. If that worked, fine. If it did not, add the smallest possible complexity, and try that.

Consistent with William of Occam's advice, first we wrote computer code that grew a tree. It did. Janak said. "The computer calculates how many leaves are on a tree. Is it right? Are we even in the ballpark?
"

As the working ecologist on the project, I said I would look into it, and went back to Yale. Once again, this seemed a simple enough question. A child could ask it. Perhaps one of the children playing with one of Jim's handcrafted toys. I imagined a conversation between Jim and his son (I didn't know if he had any children; that too was small talk, not relevant to our work).

"Daddy, how many leaves are on a tree?"

"I don't know, but I'm working with an ecologist at a forestry school. He'll know."

But I didn't know. After taking a peak into Tom Siccama's office and being relieved to see that all was well with the world – his rock collection still on the floor, the narrow path among various objects still there from door to desk, yes some of us managed with human failings and frailties.

I insent went to the Yale Library. Yale had then and still has one of the greatest libraries in the world. Its forestry school had its own extensive library. No internet, no websites full of information, just books, books, books, papers, papers, papers. For two weeks, I spent my days in the Forestry School library, wandering through dusty stacks of the main library. Books were everywhere, many old and rare, most neatly shelved, some just lying about where someone had looked at them, waiting for a librarian to refile them.

In the midst of my search in the library stacks, I came across a book someone had left out, and discovered it was a Gazetteer of Cheshire County, New Hampshire, the very county where Heman Chase lived, and where I had spent so much time in the woods. Brushing dusking it off, I discovered it had been published in the mid-nineteenth century. I flipped open the pages and began to read it. Soon I came across a statement that in one year the county was infested by "a plague of loathsome worms" that ate all the leaves off the trees. Ah. So nature suffered from outbreaks of insect attacks before Europeans introduced the gypsy moth. These were native "worms," actually caterpillars. They

did not know about *Non sunt multiplicanda entia praeter necessitatem.*
They were messy, and scattered things about. They were repetitive. I
had walked in such woods. and knew. The caterpillars in reference are
what we call inch worms. They crawled on leaves above your head.
They hung from silk-line threads so they could move from tree to tree,
and so you continually walked into them. You could hear the rain of
frass – the droppings or scat, the excrement of the caterpillars. Little
scats hit you on the head and piled, untidily on the forest floor. Dead
leaves and parts of leaves from their untidy feeding habits lay on the
ground everywhere. Wandering through one such partially eaten
woodlands near Yale, I considered my own situation and the work I
was doing at IBM.

Almost two weeks had past and I had not yet found a reference that
gave the number or of leaves that were on a tree. Embarrassing. A forest
ecologist at a forestry school who could not answer this question.
Walking along, I suddenly remembered there had been one peculiar
study done in the 1930s at Cornell University. A scientist had built a
greenhouse around a small apple tree and measured the oxygen and
carbon dioxide going in and out – a way to measure the photosynthesis
and therefore the growth of the tree. In the fall, he had cut down the
tree and measured everything about it. I dug out that paper and discovered he had actually counted the number of leaves on the young apple
tree. About 10,000. Then in the forestry library I discovered another
paper that gave the count on a large and mature tree. About 100,000.
That was it. Other scientists had weighed the total amount of leaves on
trees, but nobody else that I could find had taken the time to count all
of them.

With this in hand, I went back to the Thomas J. Watson Research
Center.

"Ten to a hundred thousand," I sat to Janak, avoiding all small talk.

"Right. We're in the ballpark," he said, and returned to typing on the Selectric connected to a computer. He was satisfied – we were hoping for precision and we didn't have it, but we had created a computer program that, in its simplest form, forecast what was known about the number of leaves on a tree. We had followed Occam's Razor. Nobody bothered to count leaves on a tree – a tedious task, and a question that only came up when you really began to think hard about how a forest worked. We had to know, because we wanted to be sure, step by step, that we were doing enough but no more. Well, we could grow a tree that looked like a real tree and had the range of number of leaves that we could find information for. Now we could move to the next simplest step: growing a group of competing imaginary trees of the same species in the computer. *Non sunt multiplicanda entia praeter necessitatem.* It worked for science. But did it work best for scientists? There was something to be said for both Tom's and Jim's offices and their approach to life. Somehow there was a comfortable feeling in Tom's semi-chaotic office, much like a forest. But Jim's efficiency was undeniable, and his mind as powerful as modern, well-executed science. *Non sunt multiplicanda entia praeter necessitatem.* It described how to study nature, but it was not a particularly good characterization of nature, not with the plague of loathsome beasts dropping frass and cutting away leaves in a forest.

CHAPTER 11

Lost In An African Wilderness

A decade or so after I became a Professor at Yale, I continued my interest in threatened and endangered species and continued to want to help save these species. I began to work with Dr. Lilian Wu. As I mentioned earlier, She was another professional mathematician at the IBM Thomas J. Watson Research Center in Yorktown Heights New York. And just to remind you, she was an expert on Game Theory, which allow such things as estimating the time for a phenomenon to continue, and she became fascinated with the work I was doing trying to help save endangered species.

As we began our cooperative research, it became clear that there were very few data about most endangered species. As I've pointed out earlier, the major problem with computer forecasts and computer theoretical models was the lack of sufficient data. We decided to try to develop mathematical theory and a computer model for one of the species that had the most data. We soon learned that the African elephant was one of the best studied, including comparative long-term studies, with lots of data, much of it then punched on IBM cards, about individuals in several African elephant populations. I was able to get in touch with some of these research centers, and one said they had a great amount of data on African elephants in one African park, and I was welcome to go there and obtain a copy, which I did, taking my wife, Erene, with me, and doing some preliminary touring of several African parks to familiarize myself and Erene with these park landscapes and their wildilife. Most important, I brought these data about elephant populations back to the United States, where Lilian and I began to analyze the data (mostly her doing complex mathematical analysis). Indeed, the data were very detailed, containing information on some individual elephants during their entire lifetime.

It became clear that more direct field research was necessary, so that I had to travel to some of these parks and do direct observations of these magnificent animals.

The first trips were fascinating, and I was able to make arrangements for me to return in the Serengeti, which had become a national park shared byn both Tanzania and Kenya.

In the midst of doing this, I also changed jobs, and became a professor of biology and Chairman of the Environmental Studies Program at the University of California, Santa Barbara. Soon after that move, opportunities arose that would allow me and a research team to go to several of these elephant-containing parks and make direct observations of elephants, in part to learn as much as possible about their behavior, and how that behavior could affect an individual's chance of surviving to adulthood and have offspring. The head of equipment at UCSB was a genius at getting research equipment. He quickly arranged for a new British Land Rover, scheduled for some other project, to be transferred to my project and control in the Serengeti.

I began my work in Kenya, then extended it to Tsavo National Park that at that time, as I said, occupied land in both Kenya and Tanzania.

I began to travel to East Africa to study elephants, and I became aware of the many different ways that people thought about nature and their relationship to it. On these trips I got to know Ian Douglas-Hamilton, one of the world's experts on elephant behavior. And through his hospitality I heard something that a long-term resident in Kenya told me about wilderness that has stuck in my mind ever since.

Ian Douglas-Hamilton came out to Kenya from Britain as a young man to study elephants. In a short time, he established himself as one of the best observers of elephant behavior and married into a well-established family, originally from France and Italy. During one of my trips to Kenya to study elephants, Ian was a kind and highly informative host, flying me about in his Cessna 182 over Masai Mara, the famous park at the north end of the Serengeti Plains, and over the main Serengeti Plains themselves in Tanzania, and going out in the field with me at several of the National Parks to study elephants. As we bounced in the turbulent air just above the ground in Ian's airplane, I realize that here again, as at Brookhaven National Laboratory and in the old New Hampshire mill, technology and nature had some deep connections.

Ian took myself and my wife to visit one of the more famous British families who had come to live in Kenya decades before, building a home on the shores of Lake Naivasha,, a large, beautiful, and rare in Africa freshwater lake north of the major elephant parks. Their home was a magnificent compound with well-watered lawns and trees, houses for themselves and others for their staff, as well as a large and comfortable guest house. This guest house, along with the main house,ronted onto the lake and was a handsome example of Art Deco of an earlier period in the twentieth century. The owner was now a widow, who greeted us charmingly and entertained us with a wonderful dinner and many stories.

After that delightful dinner, we sat outside on the lawn in the long east-African evening and this lady talked about her life in Kenya. She was born in France and came out with her husband well before the second world war, in the 1920s, she told us. "When we first arrived, there was nothing here," she said, "nothing."

An African dove sang incessantly in the trees, its song the constant reminder of the wonderful, open feel of the African landscape and its sense of wildness.

"Do you know that for the first two years we just wandered in the wilderness, never knowing where we were," she said, as the darkness gathered around us.

"Really?" I said, genuinely impressed. I looked around in the fading light at Acacia trees, and thought about the vast savannas and their abundant, beautiful but sometimes dangerous, wildlife which I had just spent weeks watching. I thought about the book called *The Last Best Place* that described the Serengeti Plains to our south as the last perfect wilderness on Earth. I began to imagine myself in that landscape in the 1920s before modern roads, with few European style houses, lost among the lions, leopards, elephants, and the black and white rhinoceros, trying to find my way from place to place, trying to avoid contact with the most dangerous of these animals, trying to find food, trying to survive. Coming out of my brief revere, I asked "My goodness, what did you do for food?"

"Oh," she said, "We had fifty porters."

And so it was and is. Each of us has his own idea of wilderness, influenced by our background, culture, and recent experiences, and therefore, with little knowledge and less contact, we imaged nature as if in a fairy tale she had described. She and her husband may have wandered for two years in their wilderness, but they were going from village to village of the porters' families, in a well-lived in, highly humanized, African countryside, as familiar to them as the European countryside was to these two wealthy Europeans.

While I sat in the pleasant Kenyan villa, thinking of one person's idea of wilderness, I thought about another reaction to nature, far away in New Hampshire, many years before. A New English Wilderness familiar as home to those who were born, lived, and worked the land and farm animals, as well known to them as close friends, well understood.

One year I lived in a small New Hampshire colonial farmhouse, a small weathered-pine-board-sided farmhouse that had been moved from far up the slope to just above the road. My nearest neighbors were Elsie and Clarence Goodenow, who were sister and brother who had never married. They lived their entire lives in the house where they were born, in Acworth, New Hampshire, running a small dairy farm. Acworth was a small village about fifteen miles east of the Connecticut River, between Brattleboro, Vermont and Keene, New Hampshire, and about six miles toward the Connecticut River from Chase's mill in Alstead. Unmarried siblings who spent their lives together was not so unusual an occurrence in New England, at least by reputation, as it was elsewhere in America.

Elsie occasionally helped out at the Chase's (my then wife's family) with cooking and cleaning, to bring in a little cash, and she had become good friends with Heman and his wife Edith and their two daughters, Ellen and Margaret.

The Goodenow's farm occupied a stretch of land on upland slopes facing south, just above a small river. A mile or so down river was an old covered wooden bridge, still in use at that time, now bypassed but intact. They had about fifty cows, and their land was open pasture mixed with stands of northern hardwoods and conifers — sugar maple, yellow birch, beech, white pine, and on the higher slopes a little balsam fir, red spruce, and white birch. The cows walked through woodlands on their ways between pastures. The entire landscape had been glaciated ten thousand years ago and the valleys were steep and U-shaped. The riverbed was mostly gravel and the water flowed clear and smoothly between the steep slopes.

Elsie and Clarence were cheerful and friendly and had that New England wry sense of humor and propensity to say absolutely no more than was required, no extraneous words, for which northern New Englanders were famous. We visited the Goodenows on occasion, always enjoying their company. Their house was an old New England style clapboard, of some no longer distinguishable color badly in need of painting. There was a covered front porch, rarely used, an old car and old truck or two parked on the grass near the house, and various pieces of farm equipment scattered here and there. The inside was small but tidy home, and we sat around the living room's wood stove, a 1930's model on which Elsie sat the coffee pot to keep it warm.

One January Sunday morning we were visiting and drinking coffee. As usual for that time of year, snow covered the ground. But the night before there had been an ice storm, when the temperature warmed near to freezing, and freezing rain fell mixed with snow, and stuck to the trees and their small branches, and for the conifers, on their winter leaves. This morning the sky was clear, the air cold, and all the trees were covered with ice down to the tips of their branches and twigs.

On the way over, we noticed how beautiful everything looked, with the trees shining in the sun, some of the iced-over branches acting like prisms and reflecting bright rainbow colors.

After an hour or so of our visit, Clarence said it was time he checked the cows and went off to the barn. He returned a while later and Elsie said,

"What's it like out there Clarence?"

"It's a Goddamned fairyland," Clarence replied.

They were never rich, they never sought to experience wild nature, but they loved the farm and their cattle and had fun with life. They were part and parcel of the nature they knew.

My thoughts returned to the Kenya villa. I listened to the incessant calling of the African dove. Many of us romanticize about wilderness just as did this French widow. But few of us have had the opportunity to experience firsthand the wilderness of television's nature programs. Fewer of us had the fortune to appreciate it as directly as Elsie and Clarence Goodenow, nor the humor to express their appreciation for something they truly loved. Most of us are urbanized or suburbanized creatures, whose knowledge of wilderness is vicarious. We are as isolated from real wilderness as was this European lady living on Lake Naivaisha.

Her impressions of Africa illustrated how important preconceived, culture-specific beliefs can be to our observations. Sometimes the preconceptions interfere with how much we can learn, as great American baseball player and humorist Yogi Berra put it, just by watching. When it comes time to discuss the true character of nature undisturbed by human influence, wilderness as we define it to be, we should keep the African widow and her 50 porters in mind, and the God -damned fairy land of a New Hampshire dairy far, as well as Yogi Berra's comment that you could enjoy baseball just be just watching it!

CHAPTER 12

When Does That Plane Land In Arusha?

There is a lot more to getting a research project going outdoors in the wild, before getting away from lions and getting as close to elephants as possible. The wonderful research done on the behavior of charismatic animals — Jane Goodall's gorilla's chimpanzees, orangutans, and Iain Douglas-Hamilton's elephants, might seem easy for them to get funding and get started. But If you read what they have to say, most began with very little funding and equipment and had a struggle to keep their work funded and organized. And I was trying to do something more complicated and less glamourous, what we were calling ecosystem research. This planning, logistics, and administration of the work was the dangerous, strange, and sometimes laughable underbelly of the research that people rarely hear about.

Having found out at Isle Royale that sodium was likely the final and ultimate limitation to how many moose the island could hold, which was part of my earlier research, I was trying to start the same kind of project about African elephants. The fun part were the elephants, but the questions that had risen up within me had to do with what qualities of their food ultimately limited how many of them there could be. It was looking at nature in the large. I had gotten a grant from the National Science Foundation to start the research, but it was a small grant as those things go, a few hundred thousand dollars.

I wasn't part of large organization that provided logistic and administrative support. I was just one university professor with a few colleagues trying to get this rather abstract and abstruse research going. On top of that, the year I was starting this project I was physically betwix and between. I had just left a position as a research scientist at the Marine Biological Laboratory, Woods Hole, Massachusetts, and was spending the year at the Smithsonian Institute in Washington, DC, as a fellow for the year at the Woodrow Wilson International Center for Scholars, on my way between jobs. The next year I was going to move to Santa Barbara to become Chairman of the Environmental Studies Program at the University of California, Santa Barbara. The Smithsonian, a center for scientists who worked all over the world, was a great help in starting this new research. Later, when I got to California, sometimes the university was a help, sometimes it was a hindrance to my research.

Just getting from the U.S. to the Serengeti Plains of Africa in the early 1980s was a challenge. Tthis was just when a war between Tanzania and Uganda had finished and Tanzania's president, Julius Nyerere, had stopped all international exchange in currencies, meaning you could not bring cash of any kind into that country, and had made international trade difficult, and the country lacked some of the basic supplies for working out in the wild.

My cooperating scientist, Jerry Melillo at the Marine Biological Laboratory, was supposed to make the initial trip with me so we could work together to set up the research, before we brought in our scientific team. But Jerry got ill, claiming a problem with his back, and I had to get to the Serengeti and make all the arrangements in Tanzania on my own. (I never actually found out whether Jerry actually had that back problem or did not want to go off the wildlife-filled Africa on a rather, from his point of view, dangerous trip with a colleague ---- me --- who he did not really trust would get him there. Several of my small research team was coming a week after I arrived, which would give me time to get the basic arrangements done. I had been in contact with people in the government, including those at Arusha National Park and the Serengeti Research Institute. Once I get settled in a hotel, the staff of Arusha National Park were going to help me get basic supplies and had arranged for a rental Land Rover and driver.

My problems began when I tried to book a flight. Arusha, Tanzania, was my destination, because it had the international airport nearest to the Serengeti where we were going to do our research. My travel agent — that's what we all used in those dark days before the internet and social networking — called to tell me that the best arrangements seemed to be through British Airways. I would fly to London, stay there at least overnight, and then fly from London to Arusha. But strangely, she said, the BA people couldn't tell her exactly what days the flight went to Arusha and which to the capital city, I was assured that there was a flight on a specific Sunday to Arusha, but nobody was certain about any other days of the week or other weeks. So I booked that flight and flew to London, spent a few days adjusting to the time difference and visiting friends, and checked again with BA, asking about the schedule of flights to Arusha. They knew no more than the BA employees in the U.S.

Once settled on the flight from Heathrow, I asked the stewardess whether this flight went once a week or more to Arusha. "I don't know," she said, "I just do this flight." It seemed extremely odd to be on an airplane where the crew didn't know the airline's general schedule; a kind of depressing sign about how the rest of my trip might go.

We landed in Arusha early Sunday morning, and the next problem arose. All banks and currency exchange officers were closed, the airport was about 20 miles from downtown, and no passengers, including myself, wasn't allowed to bring any cash with them. At the time, it was the Tanzanian attempt to prevent foreign currency exchange between nationsl I have no idea what the rest of the passengers did; probably they were either tourists to be picked up by a travel company, or locals or businessmen who were being met. I went quickly over to the only airline employee I could find and explained my problem, adding that I had come to his country to study elephants in the Serengeti. That made a difference. "Come with me," he said, and guided me out of the small terminal to the tarmac, past aircraft in various stages of preparations for flight, some being refueled; walked past repair and maintenance hangers where workmen were taking planes apart; not the usual route for a traveler. He took me into a small untidy office and explained my problem to the man who seemed to be in charge of something or other. He told me to sit down and opened his desk drawer and took out official current exchange forms, legally required in the country, and cashed several American Express travelers checks I had with me. He said he didn't usually do this for passengers, but since I was a scientist from an American University about to do research on elephants, he would make an exception.

After he had given me enough Tanzanian currency to get me through several days, I thanked him and got up to find my way back to the terminal building and get my luggage. "By the way," I said, "Can I ask you a question? Nobody at British Airways in the States, London, or even on the airplane out here knew the flight schedules to Arusha and Dar Es Salaam, which days it went to one and which to the other. Can you explain it to me?"

He laughed. "The flight from London go three times a week to Dar Es Salaam, and one day a week, Sunday, it stops here. Somehow BA staff abroad never seems to figure this out." When I have problems nowadays with air travel, reminding myself of the level of ignorance by an airline sometimes helps diminish the pain, well maybe a little.

With cash in hand I returned to find transportation to my hotel, looking with curiosity at the other passengers who had gotten off my flight and still wondering what they were doing for cash. Once in my hotel room, I began unpacking and noticed that one of my two pairs of more dressy trousers had a stain on it, and arranged with the hotel to have it sent to a drycleaners the next day.

Monday morning, the driver assigned to me by the Park Service drove up with the rented Land Rover and took me on a tour of Arusha National park. When I got back to the hotel, I found that my trousers had been returned from the cleaners. I took them to my room and removed them from their packaging, only to be overwhelmed by a very strong smell emanating from the trousers, a smell that seemed a combination of cleaning fluid and curry-like spices. The stain was gone, but the trousers not only stunk, but were slimy to the touch. I called the desk, and the operator gave me the phone number of the cleaners, and I called them and explained the problem. The owner, an East Indian from his accent, explained politely to me that, because the war with Uganda had stopped most transport and the new government stopping most international trade, Arusha had run out of cleaning fluid, so he was just reusing what he had over and over again. He was sorry but that was all he could do. Into the waste basket went those trousers.

I contacted the Serengeti Research Institute to confirm my arrival and discuss what I needed to bring. They told me in no uncertain terms that I could not turn up at Seronera Lodge unless I brought my own large tank of propane gas, because the lodge had run out and there was no way to do enough cooking and run some machines without propane. An unexpected challenge to add on to British Airways not knowing when their planes landed at Arusha, where I could cash a traveler's check early Sunday morning in Tanzania and dealing with my unclean dry-cleaned clothes. What to do?

By good fortunate, the hotel I was staying in was hosting a cocktail hour of its more important guests, and for some reason I was invited. Among the guests a large, heavy-set East Indian gentleman came over to me and said he was the owner of the dry-cleaning establishment I had spoken to that morning We talked for a good while, and since he seemed friendly and helpful, I told him about the necessity that I find a large tank of propane gas. He tut-tutted, explaining again about the problems caused by the just ended war with Uganda and the difficulty in international trade. But he said he would make some calls Tuesday and try to help, as he had contacts in Arusha.

He did find what appeared to be the last available tank of propane. By this time, the Land Rover I had purchased considerably before this trip started had arrived, and in the morning my very kind driver turned up with it, loaded all my personal possessions, took us to where we picked up the propane tank, and we soon on our way into the park.

CHAPTER 13

How Much Can An Elephant Eat?

Ian Parker climbed up on the wing of a Cessna 182, a high-wing singled engine airplane, open a five gallon fuel can with a bottle opener and poured gasoline into the wing tank. We had landed on a grass strip in the middle of Tsavo National Park, at the time an essentially abandoned landing strip in the midst of a largely unvisited and unused park covering 5,000 square miles, larger than the state of Delaware. A hot wind blew sand and dust into our eyes. I stood on the ground, handing Jerry cans up to Ian. We had spent three hours flying over this huge park and had another three hours to do, and we had stopped to refuel and to eat our lunch. Ian had volunteered to fly me over this huge park to see whether any wildlife stilled roamed its warm and dry landscape, and to see the effects of a major drought and a resulting huge elephant die-off that had taken place a decade before. An estimated 6,000 elephants died during that drought. They died of starvation, not from lack of water. The vegetation gave out in the drought and the elephants and other wildlife ate most of the low-lying vegetation. The elephants debarked and knocked over many of the trees, feeding on bark and leaves until the animals succumbed. Next to human beings, elephants are the greatest land clearers of all mammals.

I had come once again to Africa, after my visit to Roger Atwood's mother-in-law's house, this time to begin a research project about elephant populations and their ecosystems. I had come to study elephants by a circuitous route. Once people and organizations had begun to involve me in helping with endangered species, I began to think about how one might act in advance, to predict when a species might become endangered before it actually did so. What we needed was a species that had the characteristics of those that tended to become endangered easily, but was not yet so, and one for which there was a lot of information. We could study this species and perhaps developed a forecasting tool.

Species that are long-lived and have relatively few offspring at any time tend to become endangered more easily than species like rats and cockroaches that live a short time and have many offspring. The African elephant seemed to be the perfect animal for us to study. At the time it was still abundant but was threatened locally, and, unlike so many other cases that had been brought to me, elephants had been the subjects of some good population estimates. We began a study of elephants in Africa. This began with some straightforward questions about the potential rate of increase of elephants. But we quickly came to realize that elephants were strongly affected by the availability of water to drink and vegetation to eat, and so we were soon involved in a study of how changes in the supply of water and food might affect the chances of elephants surviving while they were also under pressure from poachers who hunted them for their ivory. We obtained some research grants to do this work.

Ian got back into the pilot's seat and we taxied out onto the grass strip and took off to the south, banking westward in a large circle that would take us over the western border of the park. As we flew, Ian told me about his experiences over the years with elephants. A long debate had ensured in east Africa about how to conserve and manage elephant populations. Poachers were killing them and stripping their tusks to sell them on an international market, leaving the rest of the carcasses to rot. This threatened to reduce the elephant populations to a dangerously low level. But protection of elephants in certain areas had been so successful that the animals were locally too abundant and were eating out their food supply. The most famous case was the elephant herd in Tsavo National Park, with a rapid buildup in its elephant population after it became a park. In large part this buildup was the result of the activities of David Sheldrick, its first head, which sought in provide year-round water for the elephants, by digging artesian wells and damming the park's largest rivers. The population increased so greatly that there was much concern about a possible die-off during the first drought.

Ian told me that he had tried to help control elephant populations where they had become overabundant. One side in the debate about how to manage elephants believed that the only solution was to cull out some of the animals --- shoot them to reduce the population to a manageable size. Another size believed that nature should be allowed to take its course and that, in so doing, would lead to a balance of nature that would satisfy everyone. This had been the debate at Tsavo for a long time.

Poachers killed elephants in the most inhuman way - taking only the largest animals with the largest tusks and not utilizing anything except the tusks. Ian and others believed that this approach not only was cruel for the individual victim, but also disrupted the elephant herd social behavior. Elephant herds are tightly knit matriarchal social units, with a lead female, her daughters, their daughters, and so on, as well as young of both sexes. The males are kicked out of the herd when they become teenagers - about fourteen years old, very similar to humans.

As part of my research project, several of us had developed a theory about how elephants could affect their own habitat. As I said, next to people, elephants are the greatest animal land clearers --- animal bulldozers, capable of plowing up a terrain and knocking down the trees, deforesting and damaging soils. Elephants could be what geologists called "a geomorphic agent" meaning that they could affect the very shape of the landscape.

Once we became involved in trying to understand how changes in water and food supply affected elephants, and how elephants might affect their own water and food supply, we found once again that it was necessary to get answers to very simple questions: how much water does an elephant drink and how much food does an elephant eat? Still innocent and naive in spite of past experiences, I assumed that this information would be easy to find. Elephants were well studied, weren't they? There were excellent specialists about their behavior, led by Roger Atwood whose mother-in-law wondered through the wilderness of Africa with fifty porters.

We went to Zimbabwe where we had heard there were excellent counts of elephant populations and the health and reproductive rate of elephant populations. If we could only get the Zimbabwe National Parks Department data about elephant populations, we would seem to be home free, with all that we needed to know to develop ways to forecast the future of elephant populations. I arrived one day at the Zimbabwe national park headquarters, excited and impatient to try to see if I could obtain copies of the studies of elephant populations. For me it was a tense moment. Perhaps the Parks Department would not let go of their data. Many organizations are reluctant to share data about wildlife. They are afraid it will be misunderstood and misused, often for good reasons, and the scientists who, having worked to obtained

the data, wanted to publish it first and get credit for their work, naturally enough. If I could not get the data, we might fail in our project
and not meet the terms of our research grant, nor be able to help elephants and endangered species in the way we had hoped.

But my fears were empty. After a few minutes discussion with some
of the park personnel, one of them went into a back office and returned
with a large box full of computer cards - then the standard way of
maintaining computer data - which he handed to me. The box contained detailed information about 4000 elephants that had been shot
and then studied. For each one, an estimate of its age, its health, and
vigor and, for females, whether they were pregnant and if so, based on
the size of the fetus, when they first conceived. This was a unique set
of data as far as I knew, and we returned to the United States believing
that finally we would be able to make a definite contribution to helping
endangered species. But this information was only part of the information we needed. We needed to know how much water an average
elephant drank and how much vegetation it ate each day.

Since elephants were so well studied, I assumed that for once the
answers to these seemingly simple questions would be easy to find. But
once again nobody seemed to know. We called the major zoos in the
United States, and the general response was "We just put the water out
and they drink it." In a few cases, the person we talked with would say
"say, that's a good idea --- that would be a good thing to measure, but
we never have. But we'll think about doing it"

Then I investigated how much food an elephant ate in a day. There
were several studies, some experimental, in which elephants were given
a weighed amount of food and the amount eaten calculated. . I read
the scientific papers reporting what elephants ate. But the results were

surprisingly different - different by what scientists call an order of magnitude - ten times when I compared one study with other. There were only three studies that we could find about how much food an elephant ate, and the differed so much that it was not possible to arrive at a reliable estimate of what they actually ate in a day. It turned out that the paper that gave the largest number was done by a scientist with a very low budget, and all that he could buy that could feed an elephant were slightly overripe oranges. He also chose to measure the amount eaten by weighing the throughput - that is, the elephant droppings. The overripe oranges gave the elephant diarrhea, so the scientist got a very large number (one might say this was a messy research project). So much for the science of elephant nutrition, at least when I was studying elephants.

These experiences passed through my mind as I waited for Ian Parker to finish refueling the Cessna 182. Then we took off and continued our flight over Tsavo. As we flew, I asked Ian what had happened with his company that had sought to reduce elephant populations in a human way. "I was doing this terrible, unpleasant job - killing elephants," he said, "I didn't like doing it; but I thought that someone had to do it. I thought I was doing a good deed and that everybody would thank me for doing it. Instead, they hated me. Called me names. So, in the end, I gave it up. Right now I'm now doing aquiculture - growing tilapia - about as innocent a fish as you can imagine - and trying to make a living at that."

I never found how much food an elephant ate, or how much water an elephant drank. But I learned something I had never expected: how hard it is to really do good and to be appreciated for it, even when you have the best of intentions.

Some days later, I got away from the noise of airplanes and Land Rovers and went off and watched a herd of elephants feeding. They paid me no attention to me and grazed in peace. Now and again they communicated with their noises that sound to us like stomach growlings, a low, rumbling sound. Some cut grass with their toenails, rhythmically swinging a foot as if it were a scythe, their foot making a soft, rhythmic, pleasant sound like someone raking a lawn. Others quietly pulled leaves and twigs from trees, now and again throwing dust over their bodies. The elephants seemed to be at peace and in control, neither trying to do good or trying to do ill. At that moment, I envied their peaceful lives.

CHAPTER 14

Is It Okay To Let Your Dog
Drink From The Toilet?

Pollution concerns most of us, but we have differing attitudes about what is clean. Up in New Hampshire there was quite a variety of approaches to cleanliness, food, and disposal of wastes. My mother-in-law, Edith Chase, said there was a family who lived in the backwoods who ate dinner at a large table that had drawers in the sides. When everyone finished dinner, each person wiped his plate clean and, without water or soap touching it, put the plate into the drawer, ready for the next meal. Edith swore that this was true, and she was a Quaker, so it must have been.

Edith also told me the story about the upper-class family from Concord, one of the bigger cities of New Hampshire, who had bought a summer house in Alstead, New Hampshire. They were invited to dinner at one of the local's homes not too long after they arrived. When they got back from dinner, one of their friends asked what it was like. "They was livin' just like pigs," said the Misses, "They had the milk bottle right up on the table."

Then there was Heman's sister, Mary, who lived with her husband, Walter Burroughs, in a grand brick house – the original house that went with the farm – just a short way uphill from the old mill. Mary and Walter had lots of cats, which they let run free around the house. When we ate dinner at the Burroughs', the cats joined us. When Walter finished eating, he called to the cats and several of them jumped up on his shoulders and then down onto the table and ate the leavings off his plate while the rest of us kept up a polite dinner conversation, as if nothing unusual was happening. In the winter, the cats had the run of the attic, which they used for every purpose.

Most families had dogs, and of course dogs being dogs, most of them would drink out of the toilet. Cats did too. Some cats and dogs seemed to prefer that to a pan of water by their food plate. People wondered there, as I find people do just about everywhere, if it is really ok for your dog to drink out of the toilet – will they get sick or pick up some parasite that they could spread to people?

Later, I became friends with David White, who had gotten both an M. D. and a Ph. D. at Rockefeller University in New York. Dave's Ph. D. was in microbiology and he did research on microbes that live in the soil – an intricate community of many tiny creatures that play a largely unknown, but very important role in our lives, and in keeping all life going on the Earth. It's not an exaggeration to say that for some important ecological processes, these microbes are necessary, and we completely depend on them, and losing them would make a lot more difference to our lives than the loss of some of the big, warm and fuzzy animals that appear on posters about conserving nature. It's also true that these almost invisible creatures are very hardy, and it's unlikely we could do them in. Some of them add nitrogen to the soil, making it fertile. Others decompose all kinds of wastes and dangerous chemicals. Relatives of these live in ponds and streams and are also important to life there. And then, of course, there are their nasty relatives that cause diseases. Some are good guy-bad guy bacteria, benign enough or even helpful most of the time, but if the environment for them goes bad or changes in certain ways, they take advantage of the situation and cause us and other animals serious problems. Ecologists call them facultative or opportunistic organisms, because they change what they do depending on what the system offers – a kind of entrepreneurial microbe, investing – biochemically – in what is advantageous in the environmental market place at the time.

Dave practiced medicine but spent most of his time on his research. One of his hobbies was collecting ducks from all over the world. For a while he was on the faculty of the University of Florida and told me that he lived on a street known as "physician's row," full of trophy houses whose owners were proud of them and their clean neighborhood. Dave said his ducks made him pretty unpopular there, because 120 pet ducks leave a lot of droppings, some of which cast a scent through the neighborhood that made it seem as if the town sewage treatment plant was at the end of the block.

A few years ago, Dave and I were attending a scientific conference in Washington, D. C. and we went to dinner. I asked him what kinds of studies he had been doing recently – the usual question one scientist asks another – and he said he had just completed a study of whether it was ok for your dog to drink from the toilet. Dave always had a wonderful, whimsical sense of humor, and was able to talk about the most arcane knowledge about biochemistry, soils, and tiny creatures in the soil in a charming way that anybody could understand. I thought this was one of his whimsical stories, and in a sense, it was, but he said that "this is a more serious problem than it may appear. Especially as many areas of the world fresh potable water is in getting in very short supply."

What set him on this scientific research project about dogs and toilet water, he said, was a growing number of proposals to have dual water systems. One system would have potable water and the other would have "gray water" – water that has been through, say, your washing machine or dishwasher, and then goes through some kind of filter and then is used to do such things as flush the toilet and water the lawn.

"A hew and cry erupted," Dave said, "when dog and cat lovers heard about these proposals. They started to worry about the health of their pets who regularly drank from the ever-convenient toilet bowl.' Asa result, Dave, the duck collector and expert on what happens in soils and waters, began his study of whether it was safe for your dog to drink out of the toilet.

He said that no matter how well and often you clean your toilet, there are bacteria in the environment that stay there and produce a thin layer of an oil-like substance that floats on the surface. It's one molecule thick and known as a biofilm. These films have recently generated a lot of interest – there may be many practical industrial applications of such thin films.

"It turns out that there are two major kinds of bacteria that make these films in your toilet," he said. "One kind are pond bacteria and the other are fecal bacteria." The pond types are generally benign or at worst "opportunistic pathogens" – they only become a problem when certain, uncommon situations force them out of their usual habits. Then there are "the really bad guys like most human serious pathogens – plague, enteric pathogens like Salmonella and Escherichia coli," he said. Then the going got technical because Dave really knew the biochemistry and the microbiology.

"These are gram negative bacteria," he said, "and these kinds of bacteria produce a fatty acid that form the biofilm on the surface of the toilet water. The good guy – pond bacteria – and the bad guy – fecal - -bacteria both produce these films. But they differ chemically, and you can tell by analyzing the chemical composition of the biofilm whether it was made by good guy or bad guy bacteria. Even the most fastidious toilet bowels cleaned daily contain a biofilm at the water air interface. You can't feel it or see it but it's there."

Dave got a research contract from the National Water Research Foundation to find out whether it was the good guys or bad guys who were making the toilet bowl film.

He took samples from many toilets, using standard scientific sampling procedures. This is the kind of work we who get into as ecologists because we came to the field because we loved the outdoors. He found that toilet biofilms were almost always made by the good guy pond bacteria.

Dave also looked at the difference between high flush and low flush toilets – low flush being the more environmentally popular one because they save water – "it didn't

make much difference except that the higher the flush rate the healthier the bacteria in the biofilm," Dave said, in his usual understated, whimsical way.

So, he concluded, "It's safe for your dog to drink from the toilet. And the more water you flush, the better off the bacteria. So if you're a bacteria buff like me, you'd want a high flush toilet."

As usual, Dave had come through. He had succeeded in answering an environmental question, unlike so many other ecological projects I had learned about over the years. He really knew his stuff – all the technical information about biochemistry and microbiology, he did solid research, he had his question clearly in mind, knew what he ought to measure, did the measurements carefully and accurately. And he got an answer to a question that many people wanted to know.

So the next time you see your dog lapping out of the toilet bowl, you can thank M. D., Ph. D. David White, one of the best and most imaginative ecologists I have ever met, with a sense of humor about his work that is unequaled, and a whimsical way of explaining the most complicated chemistry and biology so that even a regular ecologist could understand it, for knowing that your dog will be ok.

This leaves open the question of whether it's ok to have the milk bottle right up on the table, or your cat cleaning you plate at the dinner table, but there is always time for another research project – that's one of the fascinating things about ecology. [2]

(Sadly, Dave passed away a few years ago, meaning that one of the best ecologists in the world, and one of the few with a wonderful sense of humor and willingness to try the most arcane kind of study, is lost to us, at a time when we still truly need him, not just for his scientific expertise, but his willingness to put some humor into it, to get us away from simply saying there are truth tellers and liars. Environmental science isn't easy, and a good sense of humor combined with careful, detailed research, makes it better.)

CHAPTER 15

Guest In A Swedish Home: Romanticism Carried Several Thousand Miles

Mary Summers had been my girlfriend the entire year I was attending the University of Edinburgh and living in Edinburgh. Then her parents decided that I was not the right person for their daughter, an American student on a year abroad studying undergraduate physics at the University of Edinburgh. . I was twenty and studying at the University of Edinburgh, and was using my meager allowance during the summer holidays to visit my girlfriend, Mary, who was spending the summer in Sweden. Her mother had sent her there to get her away from me. The mother was a large austere Scot, a widow, who had little regard for Americans in general and, after a disastrous visit to her home in the Scottish Lowlands, an especially low opinion of me. I was too immature and love-sick to realize what a foolish adventure I had chosen, which is what my mother and father would have told me if they could have. To me this was all an adventure, exciting, about to appear at the door of complete strangers who had been asked to keep me away from Mary, and I saw it as if I were a young Joseph Conrad run off from his native land and sailing foreign seas. They sent her to spend the summer between semesters at the home of a Swedish couple who were long term friends, to keep her away from me.

I missed her and decided, in my then usual way, to just travel any way I could and arrive at the Swedish family's home unannounced. I had no idea what would happen, but the worst seemed to be I would not be let in the door so I would then travel a while around Sweden and then take a train across Denmark from Copenhagen across Denmark to the west coast and an overnight ferry to England not far from Cambridge University, which I had not visited, then hitch hike back to Edinburgh for the fall semester.

When I was in high school and as an undergraduate, I used to hitch-hike all the time. In those days, hitch-hiking was relatively safe (at least we youngsters thought so). It was before anybody thought about robbing a hitch-hike car driver. Not owning a car yet, I hitch-hiked all the time. And when I spent my Junior year at the University of Edinburgh, Scotland, this was my major way of getting around. It was very common in those days in Great Britain and Western Europe.

When summer came and university classes for finished, I learned that there was a World's Fair to take place in Brussels and I decided to hitch-hike from Edinburgh to southern England, take a ferry across the English Sound, and continue to hitch-hike to Brussels and then hitch-hike and take various ferries and visit with my girlfriend in a small town along the south coast of Sweden, even though I knew she had been sent to Sweden to get her away from me. But that was a romantic time in my life and I was full of adventure.

It was June 1958, just thirteen years after the end of World War II, but this fact had not been in my mind when I had planned the trip. I hitch-hiked across Germany and arrived in Rostock, a northern port of that nation, where the ferry to the southern coast of Sweden travel. I took the ferry and arrived at Malmo, Sweden, where I did succeed in getting a train that stopped at the little town where Mary Summers was staying. Of course, I had no idea what would happen when the door opened. But in my then brash way knocked on the door, which was opened by a mature beautiful Swedish lady.

She knew exactly who I was: "Oh, you are the American boyfriend of Mary" she said immediately. Then she said that my traveling all this way to see Mary was so romantic that she could not turn me away, even though she had promised the mother that she would do so. "We have extra bedrooms, so come in and you can be our house guest for a week or so," repeating again "this was just too romantic to force me away.'

She introduced me to her husband, who greeted me with a smile staying somewhat back, as if he knew there was no talking his wife out of whatever she planned. And then she called Mary and we were both delighted to see each other.

The Swedish family were truly hospital. The second night I was there they had invitations to go to dinner at nearby friends' home, and invited me and Mary to go along, where I was treated pleasantly, as just another friend of this family. A few nights following this family had their own guests for dinner. I was introduced gracefully. Mary and I had a very pleasant dinner, treated again, as if family members.

When the Swedish wife had to run errands in their car, she would take me along and told me a lot about herself. It seemed a continuation of the conversations I had hitch-hiking through Germany. She explained that during World War II she had a position with the Swedish government, which I was led to understand indirectly but clearly that she was serving as a Swedish spy of the German forces that got either in or near Sweden. It seemed a way that she could help me understand why she would welcome an unknown traveler who had come to visit her close friend's daughter.

After four days, however, she sat me down in the living room for a private chat. She said that she very much enjoyed my visit and liked me, but that her husband had said to her earlier that, however nice I was and the two of them liked me, she had made a promise to Mary's mother, and it was about time that this guest --- me --- should therefore leave. She seemed very sad as she said this but helped me pack and say goodbye to Mary and her husband, and saw me off of the train that would take me to Denmark.

Although it had all worked out to the best of my hopes, and I completely sympathized with the family that I couldn't stay long, I was very sad on the train, to the point that I eventually when into a rest room and cried for a while.

But the train ride westward through Denmark was very pleasant and interesting. By the time I got off the train at the ferry terminal, I had recovered a good mood. I was standing in line to get a ticket and board the ferry, when a young man about my age, who was standing next to me, began a conversation. We exchanged reasons we were going to England. We had a long wait in the line, and soon this young man about my age said "Look, this ferry only allows one bottle of liquor per person to board the ferry, but I have two of whiskey. If you would be kind enough to carry one aboard, we can share it on the trip. A delightful offer that I could not refuse and was bound to rise my spirits. Indeed, we two had a very pleasant evening conversation, said pleasant goodbyes at the British ferry dock, and I never saw him again, nor remembered his name. The best I remembered was he was a University of Cambridge student.

From Cambridge, I hitch-hiked back to Edinburgh and was soon settled a home with my Scottish friend, Johnny Winters. He had a Scottish Dixieland Band and we had become friends because I told him about my folk music, and soon we were rooming together and enjoying each other's music.

CHAPTER 16

Raccoons and the Great Chain of Being

One of the great ideas about nature in the classic world of the Greeks and Romans was the Great Chain of Being. This was the idea that in the world there was a place and purpose for every creature, and that in a properly functioning nature each creature was in his proper place in relation to all others and was carrying out his proper task. Of course, in the ideas of western civilization, human beings occupied the most important position in the chain. Raccoons, I have discovered, have their own ranking of the relative role and importance of creatures, but it is different from the Greeks and the Romans, but probably just as important to them as it was to the classical philosophers.

When I taught at the Yale School of Forestry and Environmental Studies, I lived in a covered barn in the small suburb of Woodbridge, west of New Haven, Connecticut. The barn has a dug-out, dirt floor half basement, an unmortared stone foundation, and two rustic stories on rough wood-paneled and wood-floored rooms. Several miles of woods extended back of the old barn, second-growth forests on rugged hills of granite, gneiss and schist, where heavily eroded garnets could be pulled from the outcropping rocks. A stream ran past the house, and a small stone dam built by some former owner formed a shallow pond in front of the house. Wildlife were abundant and it was a wonderful, if rustic, place to live with two small children. But one of the banes of life in the converted barns were raccoons who liked to get into the garbage cans, eat whatever food appealed to them, and scatter trash around the backyard. This was a common problem, and various devices could be bought at the local hardware store which were advertised to make for raccoon-proof garbage can lids. None of them thwarted the raccoons. As annoying as the scattered garbage and trash was the loud barking noises the raccoons made as they pried the lids off the cans was worse, and I wanted to separate the raccoons from their interest in our garbage.

One evening not long after dark a family of raccoons attacked the cans. I took a large flashlight — the kind powered by a lantern battery about four inches square and six inches high. Standing at an upstairs window, I located the raccoons and shown the powerful flashlight on them, hoping his would drive the away. The raccoons backed off about six feet and looked at the light for a few minutes. When nothing else happened, they returned to the garbage cans and began banging at them. I realized that the raccoons could see nothing threatening when the light shined directly on them, because that blinded them to every-thing else. So, I turned the flashlight so that it showed on me in the window. The raccoons stopped and backed off about twelve feet. They watched me for a few minutes, and then returned to the garbage cans, ignoring me. As they did so, I noticed our cat sitting on a woodpile about half dozen yards from the garbage cans. He was a large cat, weighing about sixteen pounds, and his fur was gray so that he did not show up at night. I turned the flashlight on to the cat and the raccoons immediately ran off into the woods and did not come that night. They had made clear how they ranked the relative importance of me and my cat. In the raccoon's great chain of being, cats sat in a higher and more important position than a mere person who was easily outwitted and rather slow and unagile in comparison to the raccoon and the cat.

CHAPTER 17

How the Fox Caught the Squirrel

(THE FOX AS AN OBSERVER OF NATURE) It was a warm summer afternoon at Isle Royale. It was Sunday and we had taken our usual Sunday day off from our research work. I was relaxing at our "Research Campsite," the only location the National Park Service Superintendent would allow us to camp, at Washington Harbor at the west end of the Island. Our campsite was surrounded by trees but had enough open ground for a set of camping tents and a tented mosquito-netting camp "living room" within which was our dining table, a crude picnic table. It was a short walk from our campsite to the harbor where we could, on occasion, watch moose feeding and where I had seen the moose that kicked at the shore.

On this Sunday everybody else had gone away from the campsite, and I was enjoying a time alone. I neatened my tent, a fairly unusual activity, and then sat outside and began writing letters, when I noticed a red fox sitting near a trail not far from my tent. Foxes are among my favorite small mammals. They are not only beautiful, but they seem smart and sometimes seem to have a sense of humor. Our main recent experience with foxes had been caused by their love of anything leather. An entire family of foxes had invaded our campsite a few nights before and grabbed somebody's wallet and several other small leather items which they fought over, making so much noise that we all woke up. Seeing what was happening, we chased them and managed to retrieve the wallet, a little worse for having been chewed on, but losing a few other items. When I had woken up, I saw the foxes playing among our equipment. They were annoying but they were also charming in their sense of play.

This Sunday morning, the solitary red fox quietly watched two squirrels in the trees. At first, the squirrels saw the fox, became wary and stopped their chattering. Motionless, they eyed the fox. But the fox did not move. After a few minutes, however, the squirrels forgot about the fox and went back to their chatter. Red squirrels are very territorial, and one was trying to move into the territory of the other. The owner of the territory began to chase the intruder. The went round and round, in the trees and on the ground. The fox sat silently and watched. Only his eyes moved. He seemed alert but relaxed. I stopped what I was doing to watch the drama unfolding. The squirrels' movements took them nearer and nearer the fox. Their chatter became more intense and their battle over territory more and more vigorous. Squirrels are not nearly as smart as foxes and have a shorter attention span. The issue at hand for them was no longer the fox, but who would rule the squirrel territory. The fox watched and watched, using no energy, wasting no effort. He yawned and stretched leisurely in the sunlight. But his eyes never left the squirrels, nor did he move otherwise. Eventually, the home-based squirrel chased the intruder right past the fox, within a few inches of him. Still they did not notice him. As they passed, the fox reached out a paw and, with a smooth, quick, and quiet motion, grabbed the second squirrel and ambled off into the woods with his lunch. It is a model of efficient predation. It was also a model of good nature observation. Watch quietly and do not let yourself be distracted. This is the way to learn about nature. The fox knew this well. As with this fox, sometimes the best way to get what we want from nature is to observe and wait. In this case, lunch came to the fox that watched well waited quietly.

CHAPTER 18

The Train to Stamford, Connecticut

When you are trying to understand something, especially when you are trying to decide what to do next, make sure you are focusing on the correct factors ---- what we scientists call the correct variables. In a tough situation, when you must make a quick decision, this choice is easy to get wrong. Here's my favorite story about focusing on the wrong variable, right out of ordinary life.

Harry Nestle was a conductor on commuter trains between New York City and Croton-on-Hudson, New York, where I lived when I was a child. Harry was short and fat, shaped like a sausage, but he had a great sense of humor and was a wonderful personality. He was a local celebrity, known for his continuous stand-up comic routine which kept the commuters laughing for their hour ride to or from New York City, always new jokes, always timely.

When he was not at work, Harry visited with us often and told us funny things that happened to him on the train. One evening he stopped by and told us that he had been the conductor on a rush-hour commuter train leaving New York's Grand Central Station that after-noon. At the time, there were two major lines that came out of Grand Central: (1) The New York Central's Hudson Division, which ran along the Hudson River to Croton, where it changed from electric to diesel, then on to Albany, Buffalo, and Chicago; and (2) the New York, New Haven and Hartford, whose trains rain east to Stamford Connecticut, New Haven, and Boston.

Just as the train started to move, a businessman in a dark suit and conservative tie came running down the platform carrying a heavy briefcase and jumped onto the train as it was gathering speed. He was gasping from his dash and had to sit down to catch his breath. Meanwhile the train gathered speed and was on its way north with no chance of stopping or going back. After he had sat for a few minutes, he beckoned to Harry to come over to him.

"Is this the 5:02 to Stamford?" He asked.

"No," said Harry, "This is the 5:05 to Croton."

"Oh Hell," said the businessman, "What's three minutes?"

The businessman had been so focused on catching a train on *time* that he could not get his mind off that concept. He could think about only one thing at that time and mistook what was the important factor — space or geographic location where the train was headed — rather than time, which had completely occupied his mind as he ran down the platform. "Got to make the 5:02, Got to make the 5:02," he was saying to himself.

We make this mistake often in life, focusing on the wrong factor, while the right one is often hidden from us as we are distracted. It is the source of many arguments. One person thinks about one factor and the other thinks about something else. They talk past each other, not to each other.

This kind of miscommunication happens often. Even when there is somebody as good a communicator as Harry Nestle, whose humor got everyone's attention, sometimes people are so focused on their own thoughts they don't hear what he is saying. In part it is the result of each person focusing only on one thing in a world that is full of many things occurring simultaneously and each affecting the other. We even have trouble knowing that space is the problem when we are so focused on time. In these situations, I remember Harry Nestle talking about the man who settled back in his seat and relaxed, happy to be on a train, not recognizing that with each passing moment he was going farther and farther from his destination.

CHAPTER 19

The Search For The Amazing
Triple-Canopy Rain Forest

Preconceptions that seemed to have little to do with reality entered by professional work when I searched for the amazing triple canopy rainforest. It all began when Lloyd Simpson, who helped the lady with the broken arm at Paradeso Perdu, Mike Marzolla who was with us on that trip, and my wife, Erene, and were struggling down a steep slope over muddy, slippery ground in the tropical rainforest at Monteverde, Costa Rica. The path was narrow, and the temptation was to grab onto the trunk of one of the many small trees to prevent oneself from falling down. But this could be dangerous. Some of the trees were armed with thorns over an inch long, ending in a point as sharp as a needle. The thorns extended from top to bottom of the tree. A grab with one hand would bring you in contact with a dozen or more. Also, tree trunks were favorite hiding places for some poisonous snakes. The bark of the trees contained some of the highways for bullet ants, ants about an inch long so-called because their bite was a sting that made you feel that you had just been shot with a bullet. My friend and colleague, Nalini Nadkarni, was taking us to see her research sites in the wet, misty slopes high in the mountains. She was one of the world's experts on these forests and moved quickly and smoothly down the trail.

"Don't worry about falling," she encouraged us, "the way you become a tropical rain forest expert is to fall down a lot." Soon we believed we were among the world's greatest tropical rainforests experts.

The struggle down the trail was the realization of one of my dreams, to see this famous, high altitude rainforest. Rainforests have a special mystic among naturalists. They are said to have the greatest diversity of species of any place on Earth. Among naturalists, botanists, and ecologists, they are famous not only for their great diversity of species, but also for a complex architecture known as the triple canopy -- three vertical layers of trees extending far above the ground. For years, I had studied forests in North America, and had long wished to see the tropical forests of Central and South America. That chance came when I started a new research project concerning tropical rainforests and was searching for the best location to do the field work. As part of my search, I traveled to Costa Rica and then to Manaus, Brazil.

Lloyd Simpson, a professional forester working with me, went along as well, because he was going to direct the field work we would do and wanted to see how difficult that work would be. A football linebacker in high school and college, Lloyd was big and strong and had hiked through hundreds of miles of remote country as part of our research, traveling through the far north of Canada, Alaska, and Siberia. Together, the two of us were familiar with forests of many kinds, except for the tropics.

Our hike with Nalini Nadkarni was our first view of tropical rain forests of Costa Rica. Nalini was studying epiphytes, plants that cling to trees, and she was famous for her method of reaching these plants. She used mountain climbing techniques to ascend tree trunks. Up in the trees, she found a unique, miniature world among the epiphytes and the high branches. Entire tiny communities of plants and animals lived high up in the canopy, existing on the rain from above and on the nutrients that were leached by the rain as it passed through the leaves. A trim, athletic woman with short dark hair, Nalini moved gracefully and quickly through the narrow, muddy trails, speaking enthusiastically about her work and the wonders of the tropical forests as she disappeared in the mist and drizzle ahead of me on the trail.

Monteverde, in the mountains of central Costa Rica, was settled in the 1950s by Quakers from Alabama, who cleared the slopes for dairy farming, providing today one of the major sources of milk products for the country. The Quaker settlers intermarried with Costa Ricans, and their English and Spanish speaking children grew up during the beginnings of worldwide environmental awareness of the late 1960s. Part of the farmland was set aside as a nature preserve, and it had become a major tourist attraction, famous especially for views of the Quetzal, a rare mountain bird with a long and exquisite tail. Scientists were attracted to the preserve, and Monteverde had become a center for research and education about tropical rainforests. What could be a better place to begin to learn about these forests, I thought, and especially to see for the first time the famous triple canopy rainforest, which I had heard about for twenty years.

The triple canopy is said to be one of the main distinguishing features of a tropical rainforest. Textbooks show diagrams of rainforests with three distinct layers. Photographs taken from above by people in balloons and helicopters show the top layer as an almost uniform, continuous, and dense sea of green with occasional trees emerging like islands above the rest and, in general, with the tips of neighboring trees not quite touching. Below this top layer, theory says, is another layer of dense smaller trees; and below that a third layer of even smaller trees suppressed by those above. The result is supposed to be a marvelous, beautiful display of nature's bounty. Green, green, and green, layer after layer.

Tropical forests are also said by biologists to be ancient, and their trees very old. As a result of these beliefs, tropical rainforests are supposed to epitomize another persistent belief about forests and nature in general -- that forests, if left to themselves without human interference, would, in areas long undisturbed, achieve a maximum amount of organic matter and number of species. According to these beliefs, the lack of human interference, the ancientness of the trees and entire forests, and the triple canopy made tropical rainforests so rich in species. Popular and scientific articles about these forests gave me the impression that I would find a magical kingdom of ancient trees in comparison to the meager forests of North America that I had studied for thirty years. We went to the rainforest thinking that we would see a naturalist's Garden of Eden, a perfection of nature, the El Dorado of ecosystems.

As I stumbled through the narrow trail, trying to keep up with Nalini, but also stopping frequently to look at the leaves and twigs and wet tree trunks, I was surprised to discover that the forest was not at all like the pictures and diagrams in books, or the accounts in scientific articles I had read. The forest was quite open, with big breaks where trees had fallen, the trees were not especially big, and there was only one layer, not the triple canopy. And the forest lacked the mysterious darkness said to be characteristic of these tropical forests.

When we stopped to look at Nalini's research area, I mentioned these thoughts to her. She said that these high elevation forests of Monteverde were not typical of tropical rainforests, and we would have to visit the lowland rainforests to find the triple canopy.

So, we continued our search for the triple canopy rainforest. On our way back to San Jose, Costa Rica's Capitol, we stopped at Carara, a small nature preserve that contained the kind of lowland forest Nalini said would have the triple canopy. It was near the port city of Puntarenas and therefore near to sea level. Although it was hot and steamy, we hurried into the forest, hoping to get our first view of the famous ancient and triple canopy rainforest. But we were disappointed again. We were surprised to discover that Carara looked a lot like what we had seen at Monteverde. There were many breaks in the forest where trees had fallen. Sunlight shown through brightly, and the gaps were dense with the green of many small young trees and vines. We examined broken stubs of fallen trees and saw that the wood was very soft, so that the trees would blow down readily in a storm. These were young trees, not ancient ones. And there was, once again, just one layer of trees.

When we came out of the forest at Carara, we met a group of students and their professor who had taken them to see the forest as part of a course in forest ecology. He was a professor of silviculture from the University of Costa Rica and was one of the nation's experts about rainforests. He agreed that Carara did not have a triple-canopy, and told us to go to the eastern side of the country, near the Caribbean Coast, where there were much more extensive rainforests than at Carara. Along that coast, he said, we might find the triple canopy.

A few days later, we traveled to a research station called La Selva, which means the jungle, located on the eastern side of the country, not far from the coast. La Selva is a research and educational center operated by the Office for Tropical Studies, an organization run by a conglomerate of American universities. There we found huge trees with buttresses, a thickening of the stems from the ground up to 10 or 20 feet.

Although the trees were larger than we had seen at Monteverde or Carara, the forest had many breaks and openings, many fallen trees, and it too lacked the triple canopy we had heard so much about. We asked the botanists there about our quest. They told us we would have to go to the Amazon Basin to see the triple canopy rain forest, that it was not characteristic of the forests in Costa Rica.

So on we went. A few weeks later Lloyd and I traveled to Manaus, Brazil, the famous city on the Amazon River one thousand miles upstream from the ocean, and the major jumping off place for those who wanted to visit the interior forests of the Amazon Basin. We were taken into Amazon forests by forestry experts from the Brazilian Amazon Research Agency, known locally as "INPA," the acronym of its Portuguese name. Both American and Brazilian nationals worked there, and they were said to be the most knowledgeable about these forest of any people in the world.

Niru Higuchi, said to be the most important authority on the Amazon forests, took us to an experimental area where he was studying the effects of clearings made by farmers. A field crew was felling trees, weighing them, and measuring their diameter and height.

The forest was made up of small trees in fairly uniform stands, and without a triple canopy. They reminded me more of woodlands in Virginia and Connecticut than the storybook diagrams I had seen of tropical rain forests. The trees were no bigger than you would see in New England or the Atlantic Coastal states of the United States. There was only one layer of trees, and again there were many breaks and openings. There were many, many species, but to a casual visitor like myself, most of these trees looked similar to one another, because they differed primarily in their flowers, not in the shapes of their leaves or color of their bark. Niru told us that the kind of forest we were looking at occupied 90% of the land area in the Amazon Basin. The photographs of huge Amazon trees, he said, were taken in the forests right along the river. Those riverside forests occupied about five percent of the Amazon Basin. Even in Brazil's Amazon Basin, we had failed to find the triple canopy rain forest.

The next year, having decided to do our study in Costa Rica, we began a cooperative project with several organizations in that country. One cooperator was Rudolfo Peralta, said by other scientists in Costa Rica to be one of the most knowledgeable field scientists about rainforests of that country. Rudolfo worked for the Portico Corporation, a company that made doors of tropical hardwood and was attempting sustainable forestry practices on its lands. Rudolfo took Lloyd and me to a rainforest on the Caribbean side in the lowlands of Costa Rica where we had been told the triple canopy might exist.

It was the rainy season, but the day was sunny, and so hot that the warm air steamed with moisture. We walked through the steaming woodlands, stepping carefully around large pools of standing water and over fallen logs. Again, Lloyd and I looked in vain for the elusive triple canopy. Instead, we found a patchy, open forest with a single layer of trees and with big breaks where trees had fallen over.

After we explored the forest, we came back out to the dirt road and our car. We were hot and sweaty, and tried to cool off by sitting under the shade of several balsa trees that reached 30 feet over our heads, and we ate our pack lunches. We talked with Rudolfo. I said we'd been searching for the triple canopy rainforest that we'd read about but had not yet found it. Rudolfo said, "You have, too? I've been looking for it myself. I've looked all over the world. I couldn't find it here and I took a trip to Malaysia and I couldn't find it there either."

"The trees in these forests grow fast," Rudolfo said, "Their wood is very porous and weak, and storms easily blow the trees over. Look at the balsa wood trees we are sitting under. When I came here six years ago those trees had just sprouted. Now they're 30 feet high. That's five feet of growth a year." Balsa wood is so light that it is used in model airplanes.

"Something else," Rudolfo said, "Most of the trees in these tropical forests are not tolerant of deep shade. They grow poorly if at all in the deep shade of a really dense forest. Their seeds germinate only in open conditions. In these forests, trees grow rapidly so they can gain a place to capture sunlight before other trees beat them in this competition. Such fast-growing trees aren't likely to produce a long-lived canopy, but instead a canopy that breaks up quite rapidly." I mentioned that Niro Higushi had told us that most Amazon forest trees had an average age of 40 to 60 years.

On returning to the United States I picked up a recent copy of a National Geographic Magazine. There was an article showing Nalini Nadkarni's husband, Jack, standing on a limb high up in the rainforest of Monteverde, his head peering out over the canopy. The article, written by E. O. Wilson and not by Nalini or her husband, described rainforests as having an upper canopy with emergent trees, a lower layer of trees "specialized for this twilight region" and "still lower" a layer of saplings and herbaceous vegetation. The article claimed that the photograph showed the triple canopy rain forest.

Next, I checked a recent technical book, *The Tropical Rain Forest: A First Encounter*, to see if I missed anything in my previous readings.

I found a confused message. At the beginning of the book, the author, R. Kruk, wrote that it is often possible to "discern several layers" in the canopy, but then near the end of the book denied its existence on the basis of one recent study. He equivocated.

And thus the myth of the triple canopy rainforest continues to be told, although, as far as I can tell, it does not exist in any place I have been. Like the El Dorado of the Spanish explorers, the triple canopy rainforest seems to be a search for a mythological kingdom. People I speak to continue to suggest new places to look. I get the feeling that somebody is always willing to point me in a new direction as long as that direction is away from where they happen to be. Some say that it exists in the West African rain forests of the Congo River Basin where nobody I have spoken to has been. They say that these forests led to the drawings that are in all the textbooks.

So it is with so many beliefs about the nature. Preconceived notions often dominate, and do not die even when the contradict the facts. The search for the amazing triple canopy rain forest is just one illustration of how we tend to deal with the environment through ideologies, mythologies, folk wisdom and folk tales, as much or more than we deal with it by direct observation and fact. We live with many myths about nature, and often these are told to us as if they were true---*scientifically true.* This is just one story of the many, many that the public is told about environmental issues, often told to be true and untrue, in both cases, in my career's experience, based not on fact but made up, imagination. We hear about them on television nature programs and in popular articles in national magazines. Sometimes it is difficult to tell the difference between one of these myths and the conclusions of scientific research. Sometimes scientists contribute to the confusion, as happened with my search for the amazing triple canopy rain forest.

Perhaps the most surprising aspect is that the myth is perpetuated by scientists in spite of growing evidence to the contrary. Even scientists filter what they believe they see through a blinder of cultural morays and mythologies.

The story of the triple canopy rain forest composed of ancient trees would be a fine tale if that's all it was. But our policies, laws, and actions for conservation are determined by these stories. The real world imposes itself on our false attempts at management. While the facts seem to be quite different from the myth, we seem determined to believe ideas like the triple canopy rain forest, in spite of facts, not because of them. Facts, like the real age of Amazon Basin forests and the real structure of these forests, interfere with such myths. In my more than 100 years of experience studying ecology and trying to help solve environmental problems, I have found that policies developed on myths and folk tales have led to one failure after another for natural resources such as forests and fisheries in North America. I suspect the same will be true for the tropics.

We may like to search for the El Dorado of the triple canopy rainforest, but if we really want to conserve tropical biological diversity, we must understand the tropical rain forest for what it is, just as we must understand all of nature for what it is. If we are truly going to succeed in conserving the magnificent biological resources of our planet, we must look, observe, record, count and study nature without the blinders of ideology, myth, and folktale. And perhaps, as some of my colleagues who are more expert in tropical rain forests than I, do so, they will finally discover the true folk tale that is the primary source of the story about the amazing triple canopy rain forest.

Getting the Scientific Truth

Here's a story about how some real science got done. I was asked by the state of Oregon to find out what was causing a supposed decline in wild salmon on its reivers. I held open public meetings to hear was the public had to say. One of our public meetings was held in Gold Beach Oregon, a town doing well because it was at the mouth of the Rogue River, one of the nation's most famous salmon streams.

That meeting was filled, and almost all were commercial salmon fishermen and fishing guides. When I opened the meeting, all of these fishermen sat with their hands folded or else in postures that meant they were hostile. Then the first question was asked: "Professor Botkin, do you believe that Oregon's salmon are in trouble and something has to be done about it?" I replied "I'm just a professor of biology at U C Santa Barbara and I don't know much of anything about salmon. I was just asked to run this study and I have no opinion."

Immediately, all the audience relaxed. Here was somebody in charge of a major study who was totally open minded.

Then an older man stood up. He said his name was Jim Welter. "I'm eighty years old and been salmon fishing all my life, and don't know anything about science. But it just makes sense that if these salmon are born and reared in freshwater streams and spend about a year there, and then go to the ocean and return when they're three or four, that the amount of water flowing in the stream where they were born ought to make a big difference in how many survive and return."

That made a lot of sense to me, and it was refreshing to hear something constructive, especially when I had only recently learned that the Bonneville Power Administration, which built and ran the big dams on the Columbia and Snake rivers, had spent $2.5 billion on salmon research and restoration and, according to one of their top executives who spoke to me, those dollars hadn't yielded a single sign of improvement in the salmon. How could a big agency spend that much money and have absolutely nothing to show for it? I wondered.

If you want to read about real science gets done, first understand it is not always done by people who label themselves professional scientists, especially if they work for a large government bureaucracy. Here's how a real, true people of science was done.

Jim Welter, an 80 year old salmon fisherman, who figured out how to forecast the size of a salmon run 4 years in advance. This was the best science done by anyone living and working in the state of Oregon when I was running a study funded by the state of Oregon to determine the status of salmon and the effects of forest practices on salmon.

When I began this study, I first tried working closely with the staff of the Oregon governmental salmon experts. But they did not count salmon, did not do standard double-blind scientific studies, and in general seemed to not understand the scientific method well.

Then I held a public meeting in Gold Beach, Oregon, at the mouth of the Rogue River, one of America's most famous salmon fishing rivers. At this meeting, an elderly man stood up and introduced himself. "I'm Jim Welter, 80 years old, blind in one eye, and don't know anything about science. But it just makes sense that if these salmon are born and reared in freshwater streams and spend about a year there, and then go to the ocean and return when they're three or four, that the amount of water flowing in the stream where they were born ought to make a big difference in how many survive and return."

That made a lot of sense to me, and it was refreshing to hear something constructive, especially when I had only recently learned that the Bonneville Power Administration, which built and ran the big dams on the Columbia and Snake rivers, had spent $2.5 billion on salmon research and restoration and, according to one of their top executives who spoke to me, those dollars hadn't yielded a single sign of improvement in the salmon. How could a big agency spend that much money and have absolutely nothing to show for it? I wondered. Jim then explained that on his own he went to the state of Oregon's Department of Fish and Game and got the data for the counts of salmon crossing a dam on the Rogue and the Umpqua rivers — the only two rivers where the state actually counted salmon.

Then he went to the U.S. Geological Survey and got annual water flow data on these same two rivers. If you haven't had to deal with state level agencies of the kind we were working with in Oregon, you have to understand that what Jim did took a lot of effort and time.

Then a young man who had come with Jim came forward with a very large rolled up paper, which he and Jim fashioned to the top of the blackboard behind me in this meeting room. He had graphed water flow four years before and the number of returning salmon up these two rivers in the present year. Definitely, these two graphs overlapped. On my staff was a professor of forestry at Rutgers University, who taught statistics. He looked at the graphs and was very impressed. He and Jim had a long talk, and subsequently he got a hold of Jim's data and the two worked together Indeed there was a strong statistical correlation between water flow 4 years before and the present year's salmon abundance. We did elaborate statistical tests that demonstrated that 80% of the variation in salmon numbers could be accounted for by water flow alone. Just introducing a little of the environment into the forecasting methods could make a tremendous difference. We published this as a scientific paper, but by the time I had finished running my project, I knew of no other salmon scientist who had paid attention to our finding, nor of any scientific publication other than ours that discussed this finding. This was the case even though newspapers published very positive articles about our findings.

Jim Welter's analysis became our best and reliable forecasting tool. This was the best — in fact the only — statistical analysis anybody ever presented to my committee. The so-called fisheries experts on the state's Department of Fisheries had never thought in these terms. Jim and I became life-long friends, talking and writing each other not just about fisheries but life in general, and how our common friends were doing. This is the little known story that shows one of the basic problems in our attempts to conserve our living resources, those in charge often do not have any training in statistical analysis or any methods of analysis wildlife changes in abundance. What they do need it a keen curiosity about nature and experience with some aspects of that nature. They are people who asked questions like our search for the triple canopy forest in the tropics, and, not finding answers, work things out by careful thinking and observation. That was Jim Welter, the old time fisherman who figured out how to successfully forecast salmon return abundance.

CHAPTER 20

Perhaps It Is Time to Reconsider
Going to Mars

People have talked for decades, perhaps centuries about establishing a human presence on Mars. The idea has been both for adventure and to make sure there is a second home for our species in case some disaster would eliminate *Homo sapiens* from our original home, Earth. Others have said it's too expensive and that Mars would be a difficult, perhaps unpleasant place to live, so why not focus on fixing up our home planet?

In past decades, it seemed too difficult and expensive to actually do it, but now, with: the corona virus killing many people on Earth; Ebola coming back in Africa;, pig diseases requiring killing many pigs in Chin;, international disagreements that might generate dangerous wars; and raising questions whether the human population now on Earth is too big for Earth to support. Maybe it is time to reconsider this settlement on Mars as away to insure human life persists in the universe.

Edmund Musk, of Tesla cars and Space X rockets taking large payloads to the space station, says he wants to go to Mars while he is still alive. He's not the only one, and the U.S.A. is not the only country thinking about this. Whoever sets up a live crew on Mars has the first claim to ownership of at least part of that planet — exactly how much is an unknown, of course, subject to complex international negotiations.

Space travel has fascinated me since I was a child, designing paper space ships with places for oxygen, carbon dioxide, food, water, when I was five years old and flying my paper rocket ships around the living room from one paper cut out planet to another.

I got more serious about this when I got a PhD in biology and an undergraduate degree in physics. Landing people on the Moon was often talked about as the first step in our space exploration, with Mars being the second. Another popular idea in the 1970s was to create huge artificial moons circulating Earth from not too far a distance. Among the promoters of this was a Princeton physicist who suggested that these be Toruses — huge doughnut shaped structures with an earth atmosphere, plants and animals for beauty and food. Such a torus would spin enough to create a replacement for gravity ---- pushing people and all items toward the outer walls and thus functioning as gravity. The drawings of these space crafts were imaginative, with people able to fly through the air because of the combination of the density of the atmosphere and the force from spinning made just strong enough to create a useful equivalent of gravity but not so strong as to prevent people for spreading their arms and flying. These paintings looked like a paradise.

The primary pusher of this idea, a Princeton physicist, got a lot of publicity in newspapers, magazines, and television. He said and wrote that this would be easy to do, all we had to accomplish is to make sure that any form of life we wanted up there would be sterilized of harmful parasites first.

Given my life-long fascination with space travel, I read his descriptions carefully, and his statement that it would be easy went against what I knew. So, I got in touch with him and met him in his university office. We began with a pleasant conversation and then I said that I thought setting up one of these space Toruses was more complicated and difficult that he had written. He asked me what might be difficult. I replied that there had to be an atmosphere with a combination of oxygen and carbon dioxide, at least, and that the Torus as a system would have to sustain the amount and ratio of these two gases, along with some other elements and compounds.

He replied, "I can see where the carbon dioxide comes from but where does the oxygen?" He had planned and promoted the construction of the space habitations without even knowing that photosynthetic organism — bacteria and other tiny organisms living in water or very wet soil, and green plants including crop plants, produced oxygen necessary for animal life. He was writing about a subject which he assumed one only needed a little physics and no knowledge of biology, including no knowledge of ecology. How could he, I wondered? Such arrogance from a kind of 20th century carnival salesman. I left politely.

I then got immediately in touch with Lynn Margules, one of the greatest biologists of the 20th century, thinking and writing broadly about many aspects of life and what has sustained it over several billion years (See died a few years ago, leaving a great legacy of her work to be continued). I was working at that time at the Woods Hole Ecosystem Century, in Woods Hole, Cape Cod, a very pleasant and heavily biologically influenced place on both land and ocean. She immediately said she would come up so we could talk about this, but also she was a friend of Astronaut "Rusty" (Rusty Russell Louis) Schweickart, an

Apollo 9 flyer. He agreed to come and so did Lynn for us to meet at the Ecosystems Center.

Rusty arrived in his flying suit, including a sharp knife in a special pocket down below his right knee. He said he had to do a certain number of flight hours to maintain his flying rating, and it was a nice flight to make to Cape Cod, and he had, as an astronaut and military pilot, to wear that gear. We three had a delightful discussion, ranging over a wide variety of things about life and Earth and life's history. Rusty was fun and charming and he and I became long-term friends; Lynn was already a close friend of Rusty and me. We agreed that the suggestion about a low-orbit space torus to house people near Earth was a good idea, but that we had to put the real biological and environmental requirements down on paper. We worked that out and then in a few days they returned to their homes and professional positions. We three wrote an article about what such a near Earth life-supporting satellite would have to have.

We wrote two versions of that article but found that only two very obscure scientific journals were interested in publishing it, and no regular newspapers or magazines were. We published those two, which I have continued to believe are among my least known, most obscure of any of the many scientific and popular articles I have written and published.

However, soon after the publications of those articles, and I guess because of some communication from Rusty about what the three of us had done, I got a phone call from NASA asking if I would come to the next meeting of NASA's external scientific advisory board to talk about this idea. It was to be held in a beautiful part of the Colorado Mountains, up in skiing and mountain climbing mountains, and they would put up my family with me. I went and spoke about what Rusty, Lynn, and I had discussed. Soon after, NASA got in touch with me and asked if I would lead a small scientific group, paid for by NASA, to consider biological life support systems for long term space travel. Sounded great to me and I got four other scientists whom I greatly respected: Harold Morowitz, a biophysicist who was a colleague of mine when I was on the Yale faculty. He had written about the fundamentals of physics that made life possible; Larry Slobodkin, one of the best-known professors of ecology then on the Stony Brook faculty, famous not only for how smart he was but also that he was the best stand-up comic among all ecological scientists. He had broad knowledge in many fields and about many civilizations. I invited Bassett Maguire, who was also a close colleague, whose career in ecology had focused on creating small closed ecosystems with vegetation and small animals in closed, sealed, glass containers which he studied to see how long different varieties of creatures, container sizes, and inorganic materials could persist — exactly what we needed. Then Berrian Moore, a mathematician who had recently become fascinated with ecology, heard about our project, and came and asked if he could join. Always a good idea to have a professional mathematician for this kind of project, so after we talked and I got a sense of his expertise, I said yes.

The five of us met together in Snowmass Colorado. The question was whether a biologically closed system on a space craft could provide all, or most of, the necessities of life, and whether the weight of this system would exceed the weight of just taking everything from food to oxygen along, stored on the space craft. The longer a planned people space trip and the bigger the crew, the heavier this picnic basket approach would become. Thus, it was also our charge to figure out not only what this life supporting system would be but also how heavy it would be.

As soon as we sat down and introduced each other, Larry Slobodkin said "Well the primary question for us is on a space craft, for this system that would provide food, water, the mixture of gases and solid chemicals life requires, is what should be the equivalent of the oil pressure gauge in an automobile ---- the dial whose light would go on when the system was about to fail."

That was one of the amazing things about Larry. He could take a very complex problem and reduce it to its essentials. The rest of us agreed and we spend that first week discussing what that dial would be connected to. Knowing as a group a lot of biology, physics, mathematics, and ecology, we spent the first week intensely discussing Larry's idea. Harold Morowitz, the brilliant biologist — physicist immediately got us into a discussion about what we would have to know to solve Larry's question.

The NASA scientific advisory board and NASA's administration was so impressed with what we wrote that week that we were funded for five years, meeting a number of times a year in various places, each close to where one of our five lived. We realized that to design that warning gauge, we would have to have a rather complete listing and knowledge of most of the species of life on Earth and from that we could sort down to what needed to be on the spacecraft and how the connections could be expressed mathematically so as to create that about-to-stop working gauge.

I was also asked to join the NASA space travel advisory board, which I did for several years, as the lone biologist and ecologist. That was a deeply challenging appointment, because the other members were top, well-known scientists in their field and used to knowing how to argue and fight to get funding for themselves rather than others on the panel. I was a rather innocent beginning member and, without realizing it, was easily manipulated by these super scientists, each to help one of them to pursue the search for more research funding from NASA, but that's another long story.

I've always maintained my fascination with human space travel and just regular airplane travel. Along the way I got a pilot's license with an instrument rating, and loved flying, even when my instrument rating took me into storm clouds with rather exciting rain, ice, snow, and winds inside.

When I started as a child to be fascinated by space travel, and then got directly involved with the topic as a PhD professor of biology and ecology at Yale in 1968, and also had an undergraduate degree in physics, planning a real space travel to go even as far as settling Mars seemed way beyond present technology. But things have changed very much. Elon Musk, Tesla, Inc founder and director, is producing rockets that are carrying heavy loads into space, some bringing astronauts to the space station, others scattering near Earth space with observational and electronic transfer of information devices; Micro processing computer systems make possible tiny devices necessary for space travel; Artificial Intelligence devices make it possible for machines that could be sent to Mars to find best livable places and build some of the required buildings. Books by scientists and astronauts explain how to design and set up freight carrying rockets that could make use of the energy obtainable from the gravitational fields of Mars and Earth to provide frequent supply trips to the initial human inhabitants.

And among the most important is an experiment known as Biosphere II that was built for $125 million allowed eight people to live inside a completely closed ecosystem for two years. Biosphere II experiment lasted from 1991 to 1993. It has a clear glass roof to allow sunlight in, it land area covered 3.14-acre (1.27-hectares), and it had) rainforest, an 850-square-meter (9,100 sq ft) ocean with a coral reef, a 450-square-meter (4,800 sq ft) mangrove wetlands, a 1,300-square-metre (14,000 sq ft) savannah grassland, a 1,400-square-meter (15,000 sq ft) fog desert, and two anthropogenic biomes: a 2,500-square-meter (27,000 sq ft) agricultural system and a human habitat with living spaces, laboratories and workshops. The plan was that having this variety of ecological systems would mean food could be grown year round and oxygen and carbon dioxide balance would be controlled by this variety of ecosystems. I was on the scientific advisory board for that experiment and became close friends with one of the inhabitants, talking often with him by telephone. The system is still there, the best atmospheric seal every made, and still usable.

Perhaps, then, now is the time to reopen Biosphere 2 to more specific experiments and to make use of the technological inventions of the recent decades to create a working settlement on Mars. It is a complex decision, as to whether the funding required should better be spent on the current Earth problems. The chief designer and operator of Biosphere 2, Bill Dempster, has described in detail the great difficulty of constructing a livable set of structures, which will be the focus on a separate article I will write soon.

On the one hand, a national or international project with the hope of settling Mars might be a cheerful goal as we on Earth fight against the many problems, diseases and international relations, including possible more warfare, that we are dealing with now. I hope this chapter stimulates a renewed consideration of these possibilities.

CHAPTER 21

Peanut Butter in Space

IF YOU GO ON A TRIP IN SPACE,
BRING PEANUT BUTTER

In the previous story, I discussed whether a biologically closed system on a space craft could provide all, or most of, the necessities of life, and whether the weight of this system would exceed the weight of just taking everything from food to oxygen along, stored on the space craft. The longer a planned people space trip and the bigger the crew, the heavier this picnic basket approach would become. Thus, it was also our charge to figure out not only what this life supporting system would be but also how heavy it would be.

I was asked by the National Academy of Sciences Space Science Board to lead a study about the potential ecological problems associated with long-term space travel, during which the astronauts would depend on an enclosed ecosystem for all their biological needs – oxygen, recycling carbon dioxide, water, and food. I assembled a small group of scientists to consider this topic.

As I said, there are two basic approaches: carry everything you need or recycle everything and carrying the equipment to do that recycling (including ecosystems). The choice depends on the length of the voyage because the equipment to do all the recycling is heavy. The longer the trip, the more practical recycling becomes. Each day a crew has the same average requirements for air, water, and food, so one can graph the total weight needed to be carried on a spacecraft as a function of the number of days of the trip. When that weight equals the weight of the equipment to do recycling, then it becomes more efficient to take the recycling option.

However, one doesn't have to recycling everything. Some things, like vitamins, are hard to make but small and light, so a hybrid system could be developed in which medicines, vitamins, and other light-weight items could be carried while heavy things, like water, food producing equipment,, and the large quantities of oxygen required by the crew, could be recycled. The question is: what is the best mix of carrying and recycling. Following from one study by a group of engineers showed that the total weight could be greatly reduced if a rather small amount of high protein and vitamin containing food were carried. Among the items they listed was peanut butter. So, if you're going to take a long trip in space and want to save weight and space in the equivalent of your trunk, take along peanut butter.

CHAPTER 22

The Ecology of Splitting Wood

I mentioned at the beginning of this book that I found myself living in two worlds, one "world" was as a professor of environmental sciences at Yale University and later on the faculty of the University of California, Santa Barbara. The other "world" was married to a Ellen Chase, a woman whose family owned hundreds of acres of New Hampshire land including a beach along the local lake and the ownership and responsibility to manage the gate the allowed water to flow out of the lake down a stream. Some of the stories I've told so far go between these two "worlds."

Another way that the two worlds and two centuries I lived in came together was the natural history the forests of southern New Hampshire. The forests and the trees showed me many things that helped me as a scientist to understand ecology. I and my wife, Ellen Chase, rented a small house owned by some near relatives of her family, known as "The Three Bears House," because it was built of wood including an outer layer of boards harvested from even older New Hampshire houses, and setting on a small rise on a hill in a wooded landscape that created an entire scene that everybody involved with the house thought it looked like it came out of a children's story book. It was a charming place to live with this antique rooms, except that its wood-burning furnace no longer worked, so heating was only from an old fashion kitchen stove and small fireplaces in the bedrooms and living room. Also, it had running water, but that was limited to a kitchen sink and a toilet-shower, so taking water upstairs in the evening to the bedroom was a chore.

One result is that I heated the house in the cold months by cutting down trees and splitting them into fireplace sized pieces. As a result, during the time that I lived in New Hampshire, I learned a lot of what I know about forests and trees from splitting wood, cutting down trees, cutting the trees into logs short enough to fit into a wood stove or fireplace, and throwing the split logs into a woodpile, then putting the wood into the fire. When you split a New Hampshire red oak, there is a funny smell, a little acrid, a little rotten, almost like a baby's puke. Split sugar maple just smells nice – fresh, maybe a little sweet. White pine smells of pitch. So do hemlock and spruce. Usually, the pitch gets on your hands.

American White ash – a nice tree in general – is the easiest to split. Its grain is straight – that's why it makes such good baseball bats and handles for many tools. The grain is so straight, and the wood so tightly strung together, that an ash log sometimes literally jumps apart when you strike it with an ax. It makes a nice "pong," and the split pieces fly in all directions. You don't want to stand too close to somebody splitting white ash.

The hardest tree to split is American Elm – or used to be, since that tree has been on its way out for many decades because of the Dutch elm disease, an introduced fungus disease from Asia, that arrived via a shipload of logs from Europe, so the story goes. Elm is hard to split because the grain twists up the tree. You can't make nice boards from elm. The wood grows in a kind of corkscrewing pattern from the bottom of the tree to the top. The wood clings to itself.

When I was living in Acworth, New Hampshire, a beautiful elm in the backyard succumbed to Dutch Elm Disease, and I took it upon myself to cut it up and split it so that at least in its death the tree did not go to waste. My rented house was heated only with firewood which I either cut myself or paid somebody to cut. At the time, before I got a Ph. D. in biology and became a professional biologist, I was an unemployed writer with a wife and small daughter and paying wasn't possible. Cutting wood into chunks – short logs about two feet long, a good length for firewood – was rather easy, even with elm, and especially with a power saw. But the logs were big. Too big to fit into a fireplace or woodstove, and it was necessary to split the logs.

The way you split a chunk that is difficult is to use a combination of axes and wedges and sledgehammers. First you try to drive a wedge into one end of the chunk. If the chunk is ash, as I said, the wedge will go right in and the wood will jump apart. But if it is elm, the wedge goes deeper and deeper. The corkscrewing grain expands a little, but like a green alligator, bites down on the wedge and grabs it. The harder you hit the wedge with the blunt end of an ax, the harder the wood bites back and holds on. Eventually, the wedge gets stuck and you can't get it out. So you get another wedge and drive it into one of the little cracks that the wood did allow to open, just a bit, because of the first wedge. If you're lucky, the first wedge will fall out and the second will get stuck, but the net result is that the chunk is a little more split apart. But just as often, the elm bites back on both wedges. Many times I have had four wedges stuck in the same chunk. Usually, when that happens it's time for lunch, and so I walk away, allowing the elm wood to squeeze back and tighten itself even more on the four wedges.

Taking a break helps, because then one can analyze the situation and try to figure out how to outsmart the elm wood. It's a matter of driving a wedge in at just the right angle or getting lucky with a hard blow with the ax. The problem about going directly to an ax is that the elm can also bite back on it and hold it, so that you have four wedges and an ax stuck in a two-foot length of elm. When this happens, there are several choices. One that I like is to put the whole thing in a big fireplace and burn it. The wedges and ax head come free and all you have to do is get a new handle for your ax. You get the definite feeling you have beaten the elm, and at a small cost. But you need to have a large fireplace for this solution.

Another solution is to get a sledge hammer and keep hitting at the wedges and the ax until something gives. Often the something is just a wedge, which tumbles out and falls to the ground, leaving three wedges and the ax still stuck in the chunk. The wood then closes up where the wedge had been.

Another solution is to slowly remove each wedge and the ax, by any means possible, put the chunk aside, and come back in two years. By that time, the natural processes of decay – from fungus and bacteria- -- helped a little by small animals without backbones – worms of one kind or another – I was never very good at identifying them – and insects, softens the wood. It becomes punky. It's not much good as fuel, and although the ax and the wedges go right in, they tend to go in as if the chunk were a tar baby. Nothing much happens. The wood doesn't split, it just gives. You can pull the wedges out, but you don't get a nice chunk, and if you do get a chunk at all, it burns poorly, giving off little heat and lasting only a short time. Doing this, you learn a little about the ecosystem of forests and the importance of the process of decomposition and become acquainted with some brightly colored fungi that you might never notice otherwise.

Eventually, I got most of the elm tree split and it made pretty good firewood. Not as good as sugar maple, but better than pines. It takes a lot of imagination or a big vocabulary to split an elm tree. Otherwise, you quickly run out of four-letter words and other ways to describe the elm. The two-foot chunk, that little piece of nature, is by this time a hated enemy who seems capable of many devious devices to foil a simple human task. I guess I don't recommend splitting elm wood to the faint hearted and the non-verbal.

Trying to split elm helped me understand why it made such a beautiful tree. People aren't familiar with American elms much anymore, but they used to line many a street and many a college quadrangle. They created a beautiful arching shape of huge limbs. The wood had to be very strong to hold up the big limbs at such elegant angles. It was that corkscrewing growth pattern that made it possible, I decided.

I have long wanted to organize a wood-splitting contest with my own rules. There are a number of people whom I would like to involve in this contest, people generally known as charming and gracious, but as scientists have stolen my ideas and used them without giving me credit; screwed me out of research grants so they could get the money instead; or who have scribbled reviews of articles I have sent to professional journals, writing on half a piece of paper from a yellow pad a series of invectives about me and why nobody should publish my paper, with no discussion about the scientific content or quality of the paper.

The contest would be to see who was better at splitting wood. My opponent would have to be rather unfamiliar with working with logs – after a few years of splitting and throwing wood chunks, you get to identify trees from their bark. In fact, there was a time that I was better at identifying trees from their bark than their flowers. I would select two wood chunks of the same diameter, casually giving my opponent elm and myself ash. I would go first and with a simple pong blast the chunk into neat firewood. Then my opponent, not knowing the ecology of splitting wood, would try the same thing with elm. Depending on his fortitude, we could let him go on until nightfall, and have lunch breaks and other entertainment while he buried one wedge after another in the elm.

Sugar maple is far and away the best firewood in New England, and it splits rather easily too, because its grain, though very dense, is generally straight. You can make a fire of two or three well dried sugar maple chunks, banking them carefully, and go to bed, and you only have to get up once in the middle of the night to keep the fire going and the pipes from freezing if firewood is the only way your house is heated. By comparison, white pine, like most conifer softwoods, is full of quickly burning pitch and is a lighter wood that burns rapidly. You would get little sleep trying to keep a house warm with only white pine.

Trees that grow fast tend to burn fast. These are trees that you find in young forests. They grow well in the bright light of the open area, but that fast growth gives them little structural strength and little staying power as fuel. Sugar maple and red oaks, found in older forests, grow much more slowly. Their beautiful fine grain is one result, and so is the dense wood that burns well but slowly.

For insects, oaks are the Baskin-Robbins and Ben and Jerrys of trees. Insects love oaks. Fungi do to. Oaks have hundreds of insect parasites. Some make galls on the leaves. They burrow into the bark and eat at the wood. They eat the leaves in many different ways. Leaf miners are among the most curious. They are tiny insects that live and eat inside leaves, feeding on the tasty green part, leaving the un-nutritious outer parts of the leaf, so the result is a translucent skeleton of the leaf – formed but not functional. You notice the great attention insects and fungi pay to oaks while you split an oak chunk and throw it on the pile. Also, if I were taking a break from a particularly nasty elm, I would examine a piece of split oak and admire the handiwork of the many insects at play inside.

Oaks fight back. They produce what are called "secondary com-pounds," in this case, pesticides that are not primary to the metabolism of the tree but kill or deter the insects and fungi. I have always assumed that the smell of a just-split oak is in part from some of these compounds and in part the smell of fungal decay. In any case, I became familiar with the micro-ecological system of insects, fungi and oaks, watching nature in action at a small scale. This was part of my education in the ecology of trees and forests.

Of course learning the ecology of splitting wood is a vanishing skill, because somebody invented a hydraulic wood splitter that can put the power of a Cat - D8 bulldozer against elm, and because few people depend totally on wood to heat their houses. My father-in-Law, Heman Chase, with whom I spent many a day splitting wood, invented a mechanical wood splitter. It was a cone-shaped screw device that bore its way into the wood in an ever-widening spiral. It worked, and he patented it, but you had to have a tractor to run it, and it was big and clumsy. It lost out to the hydraulic thing. I guess after 30 or 40 years, Heman got kind of tired of splitting wood, ecology or no ecology.

Heman heated his house solely with firewood for thirty years. He had converted a coal-burning furnace to burn wood. Otherwise, that heating system was a standard modern one of the time – central heating with hot water in radiators. He had a fireplace in the living room, for comfort and enjoyment as much as warmth, and a small wood stove in his office down in the basement. Ever the country surveyor and a lover of numbers, he kept track of what he used and told me that on average he burned ten cords of wood a year. That's ten piles of wood each 4 x 8 x 8 feet – a lot of wood. By comparison, Missouri River Steamboats burned ten or twenty cords a day, and usually either blew up or sunk after one or two voyages.

On his more than 200 acres of land, Heman kept sixty as a woodlot. Much of his firewood came from that lot, but he also removed neighbor's trees that had blown over in storms, or died and fell over their driveways, and he took occasional trees from other parts of his lands. I found it another ecology lesson to wander around the wood lot. This was sustainable forest in practice before the term became popular. It was a woods, all right, but to the practiced eye quite different from the other woods he owned. He harvested most species in the woodlot except poplar (trembling aspen, *Populus tremuloides* to speak scientifically). "It's a trash tree," he said, "Good for nothing." It was one of the earliest of early successional trees and grew very fast. As a result, its wood was soft and burned quickly, not worth the effort to cut when there were oak and sugar maple. It was interesting to see, on visits I made later to Europe, that much of the flat land plantations in Italy and France were European or American poplar, so deforested was that landscape and so desperate were the people for any kind of wood. Poplar makes decent shipping boxes, but not much else, at least from a New England perspective.

Heman never had to plant trees in his woodlot. One of the blessings of New England's forests is how richly reproductive they are. Seeds and seedlings come in rapidly, spread by wind and animals, and the process of forest succession happens naturally and rapidly. This was enjoyable to see, nature busily at work regenerating her forests. Not every area where timber is cut is so fortunate.

The woodlot was also more open and had generally shorter, younger trees. If you were not familiar with the ecology of splitting wood, you probably would not have noticed – it was a rather subtle difference, and the surrounding woods varied a lot anyway. But after several years of logging and splitting wood, I found the sustainable woodlot intriguingly different. It persisted; it was just different. It did have the feel of a weed lot – densely growing, tightly packed, young trees, heavily poplar, with occasional much better firewood trees coming in here and there. It was such a pleasant enough area that I considered building a small summer cottage in it. I made a clearing for the cottage, but never got it built. I think elm trees took too much time so I could never get to that cottage.

Splitting wood for the fire, one's mind wanders to such speculations. Why is sugar maple wood dense and white pine less so? It has to do with their ecological roles, their niches, and how they fit into the process of the recovery of a forest, called forest succession. That's the kind of knowledge of ecology that comes home as the blisters and callouses build during the process of splitting wood. It is the reason there is so much to the ecology of this activity. I recommend it to all who love nature and want to defend the environment. The difficulty is how to plan a future that has enough forests and not too many people, so that whoever would like could share in this educational activity, and as a sideline, expand his vocabulary.

CHAPTER 23

Roll On Columbia: Ideas
and Bureaucracies

The room in Gold Beach, Oregon, was crowded with commercial salmon fishermen and fishing guides, all looking at me with a hostile eye, their arms crossed, their backs upright or their bodies leaning forward, aggressively. I had just come in from a twilight walk along the mouth of the Rogue River, one of Oregon's most famous salmon fishing stream. The wind had blown powerfully, tossing spray from white caps, salting my face. Sea lions and harbor seals barked in the waves, only their heads visible, as if they were sitting on spring-loaded chairs that raised them up and down with the waves. Their demeanor seemed friendly compared to the fishermen faces in the crowded, overheated room.

At Gold Beach, the Rogue River splashed its way to the ocean, mixing roughly with the Pacific, neither body of water seeming to give way. I had walked along a break water and on the rocky shore. I had looked down into the Rogue River hoping to see salmon, but in the almost horizontal sunlight breaking through storm clouds, I could not see below the surface. I stood in the wind, hoping it would cleanse my mind as well as my skin, to help me get ready for the public meeting I was just about to direct.

What was I doing here, I wondered? It was the early 1990s and I was on the far reaches of the Pacific coast, in charge of a study of salmon, a species I had little knowledge about until the state of Oregon had approached me about running a project to study the relative effects of forestry on the decline of salmon, or the perceived decline of salmon. As part of my latest attempt to see if I could solve any environmental problem, I had decided that this project would include open public hearings, and the one inside that building I was about to enter was perhaps the most crucial.

The state agencies had warned me that public forums would be useless. "All that will happen is that the environmentalists will yell at the anti-environmentalists, and vice versus," one of them had said, "Waste of your time."

And acrimony seemed to have already started. Gold Beach was one of the centers for sport salmon fishing, and its constituents were crucial to our work and we needed to have them on our side. But a few days before the head of the Salmon Fishing Guides association of Oregon had called my office and complained.

"You've set up a public meeting during the day," the head said, "but we're all working people. Can't take time off during the day to go to some meeting. We want you to change the meeting time to an evening."

Susan Day, my administrator of the project, called me. "What should we do?"

"What the heck," I said, "Let's have two meetings. One day we planned for the public, and another then next evening for the fishing guides."

But the moment of reckoning was at hand. In spite of their complaint that they were too busy fishing and guiding fishermen to meet during the day, the room was filled with men who were obviously fishing guides.

The five other scientists I had persuaded to join me on an expert panel were sitting inside. They were my friends as well as my colleagues, and I felt responsible for them. If the meeting were hostile and a disaster, I would feel badly for them as well as for myself. Maybe a hostile meeting with the fishing guides could ruin the entire project if the guides got mad enough at us to seek out their legislators and complain. The wild Pacific seemed, at the moment, a calmer place than the inside of that building. Well, the time had come, so I turned away from the onshore wind and walked into the crowded room. It was hot, almost steamy. I took my place at the head of the table. My experience in confronting wildlife, it struck me, was going to be helpful. Be calm; don't show fear; be careful who you looked in the eye and who you didn't. I took a deep breath of the sweaty indoor air and began to the meeting.

"Professor Botkin," a voice broke in before I had gotten more than a sentence or two out, "I'm the head of the *Oregon Fishing Guides Association*. Do you believe that salmon in Oregon are actually declining?"

It not only was an important question, but also seemed to be an aggressive assertion by as an alpha male showing his power in front of what he saw was another alpha male. Not the best metaphors, but one that came to mind at the moment. I looked around the room at the hostile people. I looked the speaker in the eye. "We just started this project," I said, "we're just hear to learn. We haven't made any assumptions about anything. I'm just a professor of biology at the University of California, Santa Barbara," I said, "I was asked to lead this study, but I know very little about salmon and have no opinion about their numbers or the other things they were accused of. I'm just hear to learn. You are the experts."

Susan Day, watching from behind me, said that there was a collecting exhale from the entire crowd, and the postures around the room shifted. Arms unfolded; bodies relaxed, and people leaned back in their chairs. Expressions became open and friendly. A friendly conversation ensued.

A little later, a thin, wiry elderly man stood up, a black patch over one eye. "Name's Jim Welter. Been a fisherman my whole life. Just want to say that I have no scientific training, but it just makes sense, if these salmon are spawned and reared in a fresh water stream, and then go to the ocean for three or four years and return – it just makes sense that the water flow in the year they were born should have a big effect on how many salmon come back--- high rainfall leads to high water flow, good for young salmon; low rainfall, low water flow, not so good for salmon." He paused while a friend brought out some props.

"As I say, I'm not a scientist. But I went to the US Geological Survey and got their water flow records for the Rogue River right out there," he pointed to the outside, "and the Umpqua River. Then I went to O-D-F and W" – the state's fish and wildlife agency – "and got their counts of salmon on these rivers. Here's what it looks like."

His friend brought out a huge board with the two factors graphed, water flow and counts of adult salmon swimming upstream each year, with the year on the bottom of the graph. Scientist or not, old Jim Welter had looked at quantitative data. The audience looked at the graphs. All the old-time fishermen, and us few scientists. The graphs were impressive. A high-water year was followed three or four years later by a high salmon return. A low water year by few salmon returning.

A lot of discussion followed, relaxed, and animated. At the end of the meeting, the head of the fishing guides spoke up again. "Look," he said, "We fishing guides are on the rivers 360 days a year. We know the rivers better than anyone. We're prepared, Dr. Botkin, to offer to help you. We're willing to make any measurements that would be helpful to your study." A complete turnaround. The public forum had become incredibly successful, and in addition we had a great insight from 80-year-old Jim Welter about a strong correlation between an environmental factor and salmon.

Jim Welter had no ranking, as our society views these things, as a fisheries scientist. But throughout this salmon study, we continually spoke with fisheries scientists, hydrological scientists and engineers, and government agency personnel. Another part of our project dealt with what would have seemed to be the opposite end of the expertise chain – the engineers and scientists at Bonneville Power Administration. One of the ways we became involved with BPA people was over their methods to forecast possible fates of salmon.

Matt Sobel, a close colleague of mine ever since we started our positions at Yale University, Ben Stout. A Rutgers University Professor of forestry and statistics (and on my Ph.D. committee a few years before, and I, along with other colleagues on the Oregon project, were impressed with Jim Welter's ideas. We talked with him, obtained the data, and carried out a long series of statistical analyses that showed that Jim's experience and understanding was right --- there was a strong correlation between water flow and salmon returns three and four years later. Nobody else at that time seemed to have thought of that approach.

Before I started that interchange with BPA, I had grown up with the idea that this was a federal agency with a socially beneficial goal, one that I would expect to find useful and sympathetic. Part of the reason for this was Woody Guthrie, whom I mentioned in one of much earlier.

Born July 14, 1912, in Okemah, Oklahoma, Woody Guthrie became one of America's greatest folksingers and folk-song writers. He wrote "This Land is Your Land" and hundreds of other songs that are part of America's campfire singalongs. He was an iconoclastic do-gooder, a creative genius, a labor organizer, a political radical, a hobo and bum of whom one of his co-singers said "You wouldn't want to run your hand through Woody's hair, because you'd never know what might crawl out of it." Years after his death, he remains a folk legend and a genuine American character.

Woody survived the Great Dust Bowl era in Oklahoma, where he grew up, home fires that killed his kin, and knew the Great Depression from the viewpoint of hitch-hiking on freight trains and bumming around the country, from listening and talking to the common folk. He believed, like Carl Sandburg, in "The People, Yes." There is no doubt that Woody Guthrie wanted to do what was right, and that he believed that he *knew* what was right.

During the Great Depression, President Franklin Roosevelt set up the *Bonneville Power Administration* to build dams on the Columbia river system, including the Snake River. It was part of the public works projects that the Roosevelt administration put together to provide jobs for people out of work. It was also part of that administration's attempt to develop the nation's resources to the benefit of the people. At the time, it seemed a very good idea.

In the 1930s, when Woody was already famous but still quite young, he was hired by the nascent Bonneville Power Administration — it is said he was the agency's first employee — to write folk songs about the new Columbia River dams and the Columbia River projects. Woody was hired to do what we call today public relations, to get the word out about the Bonneville's projects and present them in a way that appealed to the people and made them acceptable to the nation. Woody wrote twenty-two songs for the BPA, all of them celebrating the building of the dams and what these would do for the people. One of the best known of these songs is "Roll on Columbia," who chorus is:

Roll on, Columbia, roll on
Roll on, Columbia, roll on
Your power is turning our darkness to dawn
So roll on, Columbia, roll on

The first of the great dams BPA built on the Columbia River system was the Bonneville power dam. Woody's song celebrated that dam with the stanza:

At Bonneville now there are ships in the locks
The waters have risen and cleared all the rocks
Shiploads of plenty will steam past the docks
So roll on, Columbia, roll on

The biggest of the dams, and the farthest upstream on the Columbia River, was the Grand Coulee. About that dam, Woody wrote:

And on up the river is Grand Coulee Dam
The mightiest thing ever built by a man
To run the great factories and water the land
So roll on, Columbia, roll on

In "Talking Columbia Blues," Woody said "I don't believe in dictators, but one day this country's gonna be run by e-lec-tricity." He praised the idea that in the future everything would be made of plastic, and that the electric power from the dams would provide light for the milkmaid and the aluminum industry. In another of his songs, he wrote that king salmon was going to have to give way to the big dams. It's too bad, but that's the way it has to be, Woody's lyrics said. The big Douglas fir trees would have to be cut as well. That too was too bad, but it had to be, his lyrics said.

Among folksingers of that era, a well-known story about Woody is that he was offered a high paying job playing folk-songs on a radio show. He accepted until the producers told him that he would have to wear cowboy boots, jeans, and a cowboy hat. "I'm not a cowboy and I won't dress up like one," he told them. When they insisted, he quit. Woody Guthrie was not a person to sell out his ideals. In the 1930s he joined with Pete Seeger and Woody Hayes to form the Almanac Singers, a group that went around using the power of their music to help organize unions. Woody Guthrie was not a person to sell out to industry or to be a tool of industry. When he wrote songs for the Bonneville Power Administration about the benefits of the big dams, he believed that they were good because they would provide jobs for people.

I met Woody Guthrie once. When I was eight year old, he came to our house to visit. He carried a banjo and played some tunes. He was a short, wiry man, with an open and friendly manner to children. Woody and I sat outside under the shade of a tree and played mumbly-peg. That's an old-fashioned game you play with a pocketknife. You balance the point of the knife on some part of your body — a finger tip, palm of a hand, an elbow, a knee, whatever. Then you tried to flip the knife from that position so that its blade stuck directly down into the earth. Each round of the game added another position from which you tried to flip the pocket knife. Others found Woody tough — so idealistic as to be annoying. But he wasn't like that on that day to me. He was just a simple grown man playing an old game with a small boy, a tough game but lots of fun, which we both knew.

So the involvement of Woody Guthrie with the *Bonneville Power Administration* suggests that people who believed in the people, especially in the common folk, also believed in the 1930s that *Bonneville Power Administration* was a good idea, not just for big government, not just for the big power and aluminum industries, not just for the ranchers, but also for the people and to the political leftist radicals. It was seen as a revolutionary and innovative idea.

But by the 1990s, when I was standing at the mouth of the Rogue River in Oregon watching the sea lions and harbor seals, the *Bonneville Power Administration* had become a large quasi-government bureaucracy providing electric power and irrigation water. Its large dams had

had immense effects on the environment. Thousands of miles of streams had been altered.

We were told that BPA had created the most sophisticated computer simulations dealing with threats to salmon/ Matt Sobel, whom I've already mentioned was an expert in applied mathematics and in operations research, was on my panel. At the time, he was Dean of the School of Business at the State University of New York in Stony Brook, Long Island, not so far from Brookhaven National Laboratory of my earlier days. Matt and I analyzed these supposedly sophisticated computer models. One was supposed to examine the effects of deaths of salmon occurring when they passed through the dams, as a result of injuries they suffered from the dams. I called the BPA's computer model the pin ball machine salmon game. In this computer, imaginary young salmon swam downstream and there was a chance that they would bang into one of the BPA dams. If they did, they were dead – out of the game. Just like the little metal balls in a pin ball game.

There was nothing else to the game that could affect salmon. Everything else about the environment was assumed to be constant. The scientists who created this computer game had bought into traditional ideas about fisheries management, ideas that went back seventy years but were long proven wrong. The underlying idea was the balance of nature that I mentioned before, that affected how people viewed predators and was the basis for the idea that nature, left alone, achieved a permanency of structure – that the abundances of all creatures would remain the same indefinitely. And if the abundances were temporarily disturbed, they would recover back to their exact natural abundance, nature's carrying capacity. Fisheries scientists had created mathematical models that assumed that this was true, starting in the middle of the twentieth century and earlier. The pin ball game for salmon accepted all these assumptions.

It was a strange way to think for a bureaucracy trying to protect itself from blame. Suppose you were a lawyer for BPA trying to make it look as if the agency's effect on salmon was unimportant. To do this, you would hire scientists to create a model with all the qualities of the environment that they could think of varying – water flow, temperature, amount of gravel, ocean currents, numbers of predators. With all these things changing all the time, the effects of a few young salmon banging their heads against the dams would look small. Instead, the BPA scientists has created an imaginary model that made the BPA appear to have the greatest possible effect on the salmon. The irony was that the assumptions were wrong. But the sad consequence was that, locked into old ways of thinking, these scientists could not find a way to understand how salmon really worked their way through life, and what actually affected their survival.

Strangest of all, they had never done what Jim Welter had accomplished – never graphed the flow of water against the returns of salmon three years later. I puzzled about why not a single scientist working for this huge bureaucracy thought of that straightforward idea? I spoke with Jack Robertson, then one of the vice-presidents of the BPA. He was planning on retiring and was thinking about a new career in an environmental field. He wanted to help improve the environment. He told me that he wasn't a scientist, and that he had had to take the advice and statements of the BPA's scientists about what was happening with the salmon and what to do about it. Salmon were in trouble, the trouble that Woody Guthrie's lyrics had forecast. BPA and many other government agencies were spending a lot of money to try to improve things and to meet the requirements of the Endangered Species Act.

Jack said that nothing they had tried had worked — that the $120 million a year the BPA was spending on salmon research and restoration had not led to a *single* sign of improvement. More than an equivalent to a billion dollars today.

How could this be? Jack was a well-meaning person, a good person. From the time of Woody Guthrie to Jack Robertson, people working for BPA -- at least the ones I had met -- meant well and tried hard. Disputes over environmental issues are often portrayed as a battle between good and evil -- the good and evil depending on which side of the issue one is on. But this was not a case of good versus evil. It didn't take good and evil people to create a bad situation. There was something about the situation that our society had set up that was causing the problems. As long as we believed that what was happening was *only* the result of one side being made up of good people and the other of evil, we would miss what the real causes were.

If anything, Woody Guthrie suffered from the arrogance of believing he knew the TRUTH with capital letters, and that such complex systems as human society and ecosystems could be reduced to simple solutions. He did not suffer from ignorance of the consequences of the dams on the environment, he just believed that the needs of the people were to be met from jobs created by the new dams and that the people would benefit from electricity more than from salmon and Douglas fir.

From its start as a new, innovative idea, BPA had grown into a culture that had become fixed in its beliefs, so that the agency suffered from paradigms of pervading natural resource management and bureaucratic inertia.

BPA was caught in a double bind. It had become a huge bureaucracy trying to survive. And it had bought into outdated and wrong scientific beliefs, also fossilized, hardened within a certain scientific community that held its ideas captive.

In every government agency I have worked with, there are people who were trying to do the best job possible, to solve the problems. But the system works against them. The challenge to our democracy -- to western civilization and for nature -- is to find a way to maintain flexibility as knowledge, needs, and desires change. The challenge for the Columbia - Snake River System was to find a way to develop flexibility in both science and management that considered new findings of science and the present needs and desires of the people of America.

In this case, it seemed that the good idea of the 1930s, a way to bring power and water to the people, had worked out quite the way it was supposed to. It seemed that someone had started with a good idea, but that our society had ended up with a large bureaucracy. Woody Guthrie certainly hadn't intended it to turn out that way, as far as I could tell. But a large bureaucracy seemed limited in its ability to deal with nature, not able to sponsor the kind of creative insight that might come to a long-time fisherman who had a natural sense of curiosity and a bent toward quantitative analysis.

Jim Welter was like Heman Chase, both careful observers of their surroundings, careful thinkers about it, fascinated by it and trying to do their best, working mainly on their own or in small groups. Maybe it was better to be like the fox, acting alone, then like the squirrels at Isle Royale, confused by their internal squabbling and concerns.

CHAPTER 24

How the Coyotes Outwitted
A Bureaucracy

Big predators seem to have always posed a dilemma to people. Whether it has been lions, leopards, tigers, sharks, wolves, or sea lions, one prevailing attitude has been that the only good varmint is a dead varmint. On the other hand, people have had a certain respect, even admiration, for the skills of these predators, and for their cleverness.

The stealthfulness and secretiveness of some of the big predators is legendary, and a subject for admiration. The most impressive story about the ability of a big predator to keep out of sight is the story of a female mountain lion in Glacier National Park. The National Park Service staff began to notice mountain lion tracks right in the middle of main tourist visiting areas of the park, where the lodges and staff housing was. The tracks appeared overnight and began to occur with such frequency that the rangers decided they had better track down the lion and move it far away. They started tacking it and discovered that it was a female who had a den with a cub in it underneath the porch of one of the park employees. Their stealth and ability to fool the "expert" ranger illustrates one of the reasons mountain lions can survive and prevail. It also illustrates how easily wildlife experts can be fooled.

But of course the wiliest and smartest of all animals of North America seems to be the coyote, known to science as *Canis latrans*, that is, as a member of the dog genus and more to the point, capable of interbreeding with domestic dogs, the offspring of which are known as coydogs. And among the clever, the American coyote seems to top the list. The coyote has been a major symbolic animal in the myths of Native Americans of the southwest, the Great Plains, and California. The coyote is known in these cultures as the magician and trickster, as well as a creator, sometimes as the agent who brought people fire, daylight, and arts. Since European settlement of North America, he is known mostly as a varmint, a pest to be exterminated. The coyote is infamous for the difficulty of finding a way to kill it, and even when this has been successful here and there, the total numbers of coyotes only seem to increase and the range of the coyote to have spread. The coyote gets its name from the Aztec *coyotl,* indicative of its wide range – it ranges from Costa Rica north to Alaska. Once known as an animal of the American west, in recent decades it has moved eastward and is now found in many east coast's states And today, coyotes are familiar in city parks, especially because the Corona Virus is keeping human visitors to these park way down.

Original associated with the great outdoors, It is found today within the suburbs of Los Angeles, in downtown San Francisco, where it comes into neighborhood parks, and has learned how to ask people for food ---- politely and without threat ---- while also on its own time hunting any local small mammals. My daughter, Nancy, who lives near one of these parks, often sees one or two coyotes, sometimes simply passing close to her on a narrow trail, smart enough to appear friendly and perhaps giving a kind of wishful look as if politely asking for a snack. She is told by the city park officials that there is no point is trying to get rid of these coyote park visitors, because if you kill one, there are enough in the distance of the suburbs that each dead coyote will soon be replaced by another live one.

Not only is the coyote wily, but it is also fast, said to be able to make a dash toward a prey at forty miles an hour. One thing seems certain: these animals seem experts at what they do, including their ability to outwit bureaucracies as well as experts in predator control, naturalists, ecologists, ranchers, hunters, and just plain tourists.

For an exceptionally long time, predator control dominated government policy and pioneer practice in America. When the east coast of America was still a colony of Great Britain, various states enacted laws that provided bounties for the pelts of wolves. But as the numbers of these animals declined, respect for them and their persistence has grown, and most big predators are either listed as endangered under the U S Endangered Species Act or else subject to special attempts to help them. As early as about 1912, the Bureau of Biological Survey, the predecessor to the Fish and Wildlife Service, was given the job of controlling predators out west. From then to the mid-1970s the activity continued.

Aldo Leopold, later to become famous as one of the most important proponents of conservation of nature, began his career in predator control, and his early writings were anti-predator. He was working with the then *U.S. Bureau of Biological Survey,* which was simply following the conventional wisdom of the time. (It was soon to become the *U. S. Fish and Wildlife Service* and, over the years, develop the same kind of fixed tendencies that had happened to the Bonneville Power administration.)

During the time I was working on the salmon problems in the Pacific Northwest, I visited with Lee Talbot, one of the members of the panel of scientific experts that I had set up for that project. Lee was the one who had told Richard Needles about the social behavior of gazelles in Africa, which Needles then translated into the story about the social behavior of sperm whales.

We were standing at the Sommette Automobile Race Tract in West Virginia, about an hour and a half's drive from Lee's home in McLean, Virginia, (because in addition to being one of the top ecologists in the United States, Lee was also a champion car racer.) We got talking about the dilemma of big bureaucracies. Racing cars roared round the track, gears whining, exhausts thundering. Conversation stopped each time a car ran by the starting gate not far from where we stood next to Lee's Formula Ford. Lee had needed an extra hand and I had come along to help push and shove and hold things, while he and his chief mechanic made subtle adjustments to the machine and checked its safety.

Lee was then and still is one of the world's experts on wildlife conservation and one of the most successful in getting things done, leaving a mark on the world, making it a better place. Lee had extensive experience in government. He worked in the *Council of Environmental Quality* under the Nixon and Carter administrations. He helped write the *Endangered Species Act* and the *Marine Mammal Protection Act*. He had worked in 120 nations on the conservation of nature for the World Bank and at one time was head of the *International Union for the Conservation of Nature*. Lee was well known as one of America's leading thinkers and actors for the environment.

In addition to our love of the outdoors and our work to help conserve nature, Lee and I shared an interest in modern technology and in fast moving vehicles (mine being airplanes. I flew small single-engine airplanes and had an instrument rating so I could and did fly through storms with ice, snow, wind, and rains). Our friendshipgrown out of discussions about both. I flew small airplanes and Lee raced cars. Lee was a world champion race car driver, having won or come in second in famous international events like the cross-Africa rally. And for several decades he was a consistent winner in the United States race car circuit. I had never even considered trying a fly in an airplane race, but Lee not only participated, he had made a science out of understanding how to win and he did win, most of the time. He knew how to get things done on the racetrack. His mechanic was also an expert at keeping automobiles on the move. Nobody thought I was an expert about anything at the racetrack – I was just the equivalent of a hired hand, someone to go and fetch or to pass a tool or help drive the vehicle that pulled the race car.

As he prepared his Ford for the next race, Lee talked about his perceptions of big bureaucracies. He saw a historical pattern in the development of government agencies. "A new idea becomes popular. People become outraged over the way things have been going following old ideas," Lee said. "Elected politicians respond by establishing a new government agency. That agency creates a need for a new kind of expert, and the agency has money. Universities recognize the new public need and the new money. New university departments and schools are established. Universities train the professionals required by the new government agencies. The universities and the government agencies benefit. So do the university faculty. They get their research grants funded and research papers published. Faculty, universities, and agencies come to have common, vested interests in maintaining the status quo. University faculty established a set of ideas and methods. These became the standards in use by the practitioners. The government agencies rely on the professionals from the universities for advice, and the university and the faculty rely on the government for funding. Practices, ideas, and approaches become fixed. What had been a new idea becomes societal inertia." He stopped talking while several cars roared by.

"Eventually, because people are imperfect and our ideas and forecasts are never perfect," Lee continued, "the bad as well as the good of what were social innovations become apparent. Citizens become upset by the bad effects. A new outcry begins, politicians respond, and the cycle starts again."

"Perhaps experts in political science will find this explanation incredibly naive and simplistic, but for those of us working in the trenches, trying to find real solutions to real problems, that analysis fits," I said, "The way I put it is: you start with a good idea and you end up with a bureaucracy – just like Woody Guthrie and the Bonneville Power Administration."

[3] "I'll tell you about my own experience in getting things down in spite of the tendencies of bureaucracies to become fixed in their ideas," Lee said. "Early in my career – in the summer of 1948 – I worked as a state biologist in California at *San Joaquin Experimental Range*, run by United States *Forest Service* and the *University of California at Davis*. Although the experimental range was on Forest Service land, the university did a lot of the research there. This was my first acquaintance with a poison known as 1080 that was used to control predators and

rodents – control in this case being a euphuism for kill." It was the same poison that was used in California and many had blamed for some of the deaths of the endangered California condors when those birds flew in the wild.

"The university was conducting experiments to see how far through an ecosystem food chain and within the cycling of chemicals in an ecosystem this poison, 1080, went," Lee continued. "In theory, such poisonous organic compounds were supposed to decompose in their first victim, but it seemed that 1080 could kill a target animal and then remain poisonous and kill any animal that fed upon the one it had just killed. If you put out seeds with 1080 in it, you killed birds – any seed-eating birds. If you put out grain with 1080 to kill rodents, you would also kill birds, including raptors like hawks and eagles that fed on the dead rodents, and scavengers like turkey vultures that ate the carcasses."

From that summer experience, Lee became impressed with how dangerous this chemical was to an ecosystem, not just the target animals. In the years afterward, he saw the same food chain effects with other poisonous put out to kill varmints, and he became concerned with the widespread use of any broad spectrum poisons, especially in the western states.

The predator control experts, most of whom work for the *U. S. Fish and Wildlife Service* or for state agencies (and were known as gopher-chokers) operated as "laws unto themselves, regardless of land owners," Lee said. "Over the years it became clear that predator control operations of the government were not under control, and the biologists and control officers involved seemed to have little idea what impact they were having," he said.

At the time, poisoning predators and prairie dogs and other rodents was popular with some ranchers —-- including the more powerful rancher groups. "Like any bureaucracy, the Fish and Wildlife Service predator control people pretty soon lost view of the finer points of their mission," Lee said, "and simply turned it into a way of expanding their endeavors – the more they could kill, the bigger the body count, the better for them within their system – more jobs for them, more money to spend, more influence. So, they went about their business without much of a scientific basis."

We strolled over to his car to watch what his mechanic was doing. Lee stepped into his car transport trailer and brought out some tools that he handed to the mechanic. "All sorts of devices were tried on the coyote," Lee continued. "One was the coyote getter – a shotgun cartridge buried in the ground with just top showing, a powder charge in bottom of the cartridge and a charge of stricken or 1080 at the top. A piece of cloth soaked in a coyote attractor —-- some kind of bait sat on top of the cartridge, connected to it. When the cloth was pulled, the cartridge fired the poison into puller's mouth." The intention was that a coyote would be the puller.

"Another method was simply to throw poisoned bait out of airplanes -- tons of poisons were released indiscriminately this way, especially for rodent control, in poisoned on grain."

Lee had waited for a number of years to do something about this. In the early 1970s, when I was trying to learn how long a whale slept, how many leaves were on a tree, and was roaming forests of New Hampshire with my father-in-law and beginning to study wilderness and to try to help save endangered species, Lee took a more direct approach. He joined the staff of the newly created *Council on Environmental Quality*, a new part of the executive branch of the federal government, formed during the Nixon administration. Several things came together about this time. First, the increase in public concern with the environment meant that it might be possible to educate the public about the role of predators in nature, and the degree to which they were or were not varmints. Second, President Nixon recognized the growing public interest in environment and believed that there could be political advantages for him to do good things about the environment. The question was: what things? His aides, Erlichman and Halderman, were actively looking for politically visible good things to do for the environment. Third, the staff of CEQ was looking for effective, scientifically sound things to do for the environment.

At long last there seemed to be possibility about doing something to stop the use of 1080, but there was concern about the power of western stockman and the employees of the *U. S. Fish and Wildlife Service*. "To get something done in our nation, you need a triggering event – something that grabs the public's attention and creates an opportunity for political action, because the action will show that the politician is listening to and responding to the needs of the people," Lee told me. And you had to wait and watch for the right event. It reminded me of the fox on Isle Royale watching and waiting out the squirrels, waiting for just the right time for action.

"With 1080, the trigger was the day that a young boy shot himself in the face with a coyote-getter," Lee continued. "He was on a camping trip out west with his family and came across a piece of cloth lying on the ground. Typical of a young boy, his curiosity was aroused, and he pulled on the cloth. The shotgun cartridge exploded and fired 1080 onto the boy's face. He was okay, but the event got a lot of media attention. A young boy shot with a poison from a device set out by a federal government agency to kill coyotes."

Lee's mechanic motioned for us to help him push the Formula Ford to a better location for him to work underneath it, and we helped him, continuing our conversation as we gently pushed the light vehicle.

"A second triggering event added to the situation: a series of eagle killings out west came to light," said Lee. "One of the federal predator control people had been taking local ranchers up in an airplane so that they could shoot and kill eagles. This was in direct violation of two federal laws, one a special act to protect the eagle, America's symbolic bird, and the other the Endangered Species Act."

"They and the ranchers argued that eagles were threat to livestock. Eagles were believed to be able to kill calves and newborn sheep – an unlikely event, considering the relative size of an eagle and a calf, and a calf's mother."

This was a continuation of the persistent belief that the only good varmint was a dead varmint. "The intentional violation of two federal laws by zealous federal predator control experts hit the national press, creating public concern. Major national environmental organizations jumped on this event."

Lee told me that he used the two triggering events and prepared a proposal for the White House that took into account public outrage over the injured young boy, the illegal killing of eagles, and long-term environmental concerns about the release of broad spectrum poisons into the environment, poisoning the west, and resulting in uncontrolled killing of predators.

Nixon saw the then newly growing public concern about the environment as an opportunity, and as I said he was looking for an event that would make a positive image for him about environmental issues. Lee was able to use the idea that elimination of 1080 and the uncontrollable weapons that involved this poison could be such an action – that the national outrage provided Nixon with a politically good thing he could do.

The question was how to put this into action, given strong political opposition in the west and from the ranchers' congressional representatives, as well as from the predator control people and their allies in Department of Interior. Lee got together with Nat Reed, then Assistant Secretary of Interior for fish, wildlife, and parks, who was also concerned about the unnecessary killing of predators and the unannounced spreading of poisons into the environment. "It would be typical for a large federal bureaucracy to close ranks behind the predator control people," Lee told me, "but Nat was an exception."

Nat and Lee recognized that they needed an impeccable scientific rationale – they needed the blessings of the right kinds of experts. They considered forming a National Academy of Sciences panel to examine predator control and the use of broad-spectrum poisons. But they decided that this would take too long so that the advantages of the triggering actions would be lost. Instead they put together an expert committee of top authorities on predators and on the impact of predators on their ecosystems. Stanley Cain, a well-known scientist, who had been Dean of the School of Natural Resources at the University of Michigan, headed the committee. "His credentials as an environmental scientist were impeccable," Lee explained.

Other members of the panel included Starker Leopold, Morris Hornknocker (known as the world's top big-cat biologist); and Fred Wagner, a professor at Utah State University, who had done much work with the livestock industry. They were asked to assess all available information about the impact of predator and rodent control operations in the west, and report back with recommendations about what ought to be done. Lee made clear that the panel was completely independent, and that Lee and Nat should not have any additional contact with its members until they study was completed, so that it would be fair and impartial. The panel held hearings around the west.

The Cain Committee provided an independent, scientific impeccable report. The report stated that "committee found that consistent poisons had been applied to range and forest lands without adequate knowledge of how they affect the ecology or whether

'they actually prevent loss of livestock". They went to state that "Large scale use of poisons . . . has unintentionally had effects on" non target animals. One finding was that it wasn't possible to identify what the actual total impact of the indiscriminate release of poisons, but that since this release did not seem successful against coyotes, therefore much was being down with no knowledge of effect even on the livestock that it was being done to save."[4]

Thus the Cain Committee, as it came to be known, reported as its key findings: vast amounts of poison were being applied indiscriminately in the west, including out of airplanes, with no control and no idea of the real impact. They had data on killing of nontarget species including endangered species, and the role of the predator control people in extermination the wolf, grizzly bear, and mountain lion from most of their ranges.

With this independent assessment, Lee wrote up an executive order for Nixon to issue. The arguments presented to Nixon in a brief decision paper (Nixon said he would not read anything longer a page, and better only a paragraph.) Nixon saw this as an opportunity and issued an executive order #11643 in 1972 titled "Environmental safeguards on activities for animal damage control on federal lands." The important statement is the policy in section 1. "It is the policy of the Fed govt to (1) restrict the use on federal lands of toxic substances for the purpose of killing predatory mammals or birds" (2) restrict the use on such lands of chemical toxicants which caused any secondary poisoning effects for the purpose of killing other mammals, birds or reptiles." (This gets at the rodent control.) (3) restrict use of both types of toxicants in any federal programs of mammal or bird damage control that may be authorized by law." (This stops activities off of federal lands.)

Lee began to get ready for the next race. He brought out his fire-retardant coverall and started to get into them. "The report also goes on to state that 'All such mammal or bird programs shall be conducted in a manner which contributes to the maintenance of environmental quality and to the conservation and protection to the greatest degree possible, of the nation's wildlife resources, including predatory animals.' Lee reached for his helmet. "In the president's message on the environment made public on February 8, 1972, Nixon said that 'Americans today set high value on the preservation of wildlife. The old notion that 'the only good predator is a dead one' is no longer acceptable as we understand that even the animals and birds which sometimes prey on domesticated animals have their own value in maintaining the balance of nature.'

The executive order barred the use of poisons for predator control on all federal lands with very few exceptions, and in all federal programs, whether they were on public or private lands. EPA suspended and cancelled poisons used in predator control.

Here was an example of a success story. How had Lee done it? The basic elements involved applying scientific knowledge. This required an excellent scientific assessment by a group of scientists who would be recognized as experts. But to make the whole thing work, one had to take advantage of crucial timing. This means that Lee had to have his own policy lined up, and then he was in a position to do something to do about it. He had to understand the opposition, and had to have worked out the plan of action in advance, and then – when the opportunity arrived – was able to put the plan into operation quickly, in this case getting White House approval and lining up as much scientific backing as possible.

It was a relief to hear of such a success story in conserving nature. On the other hand, no one has yet figured out how to control coyotes when they are pests, and sometimes they are, just as raccoons in my garbage cans were in home when I was on the Yale faculty in Woodbridge, Connecticut. The success, like all things in the real world, had its limits. Because Nixon's action was an executive order rather than a congressional law, it could be reversed by subsequent Presidents. And President Reagan did this – he brought back the use of 1080, so it became a problem with the condors in the 1980s.

As Lee climbed into his fireproof coverall, sat down in his race car and put on his seat belt, he reminded me that such successful action requires a triggering event, and that you have to be ready to act —– to have the scientific understanding available. His story also made clear that it wasn't easy to bring out policy that helped nature, and it took a combination of applied science, scientists, and a lot of political savvy. It was the way Lee had succeeded in getting things done in government and it was the way he approached racing and winning races in his formula Ford. His engine started and we put our fingers against our ears and watched him drive slowly out to the track.

CHAPTER 25

How Many Bowhead Whales Ever
Lived On The Earth?

We struck that whale and the lines paid out And she gave
a flourish with her tail And the boat capsized, and we
lost our darling boys And we never caught that
whale, brave boys, Never caught that whale.
From *Greenland Fisheries*, an American Folksong

Back to my days working in Woods Hole, one day I was eating lunch
at the Fishmonger restaurant, a common gathering place in a weather-
worn building just by the lift bridge that led into Eel Pond, the pond
in the center of Woods Hole that served as a marina and was where the
Alvin, a then famous deep sea diving vessel, was docked. You could
just see the pond and the bridge out the smudged, dirty windows of
the restaurant. I sat at one of the rough-hewn, splintery wooden tables
in the dimly lit room. The restaurant was full of its usual crowd, a mixture of students, graduate students, research scientists, but few tourists.
Dress was the Woods Hole usual --- a reverse status dress code ---
grubby was good; grudge was anticipated here by several decades. The
general attitude was that the more important you were the sloppier you
could and should look. My wife, Erene, who tried to dress nicely, in a

business-like manner for her work at the Laboratory, knew she was criticized for her careful and neat appearance, and people assumed she must be a secretary, as only secretaries dressed as well.

Fall weather was turning and the damp coldness contrasted with the dry heat of the African plains I had just visited. The neat, starched, khaki uniforms of East African park staff and scientists, shorts and high socks, were replaced by aging blue jeans.

The food was pretty good and relatively cheap, and the Fishmonger was a popular spot with the scientists and students. I was musing about the many things that had nothing to do with science kept interfering with attempts to apply science to wildlife, endangered species, to eco-systems, to life on the whole Earth. Superficial beliefs, going as far as how one looked and dressed, could often determine whether work was taken seriously.

I was trying to relax and enjoy a bowl of clam chowder when Fred, one of my research assistants, hurried in and sat down next to me, a little out of breath. "You've got a strange visitor," he said, "Nobody knows what to make of him, but he insists on speaking with you."

"What's the problem?" I asked.

"He's in a three-piece pinstriped suit, is what," said Fred, "hand-kerchief in his pocket. Wearing those rimless glasses. Has a shiny leather briefcase, polished leather shoes. We think he must be a typewriter salesman, but then why would he want to see you? Anyway, he seemed determined and he's waiting at your office. We didn't know what to do. Some kind of freak." Fred said. "Obviously, a wimp, no way a marine biologist. He insisted on seeing you and not the purchasing officer."

"Doesn't sound so bad," I said.

"Remember, Dan, some of the old-time marine biologists already think you're a little weird, working at MBL and going to Africa to study elephants. Don't push your luck. Word to the wise. The word is out that nobody can understand what you're really doing here, what with computer whale games and experts on elephants coming to visit. Best to get this typewriter salesman out the door." I hurriedly finished my clam chowder and bread and herb tea and went back to my office, at Fred's insistence.

Just as Fred as described him, my visitor was elegantly and smartly dressed, a tall man who stood just inside my office looking around. I was suddenly conscious of my messy office, still cluttered with papers and still decorated only by the one lonely Christmas cactus still surviving in a dingy corner on top of a bank of file cabinets. My office had the drab color of Jim Janak's combined with the confusion of Tom Siccama's, lacking only piles of rocks and boulders on the floor. This spiffy gentleman introduced himself.

"John Bockstoce, anthropologist, New Bedford, Massachusetts Whaling Museum." He handed me a business card and looked around for a place to sit. I hastily moved a pile of papers from an old wooden armchair and, dusting it quickly with them, offered him a seat. He carefully took off his elegant gray pin-striped suit coat and hung it on the back of the chair, first dusting the chair. As he did so, I noticed that large muscles bulged from his upper arms and torso, pushing against starched his white shirt.

Once he settled into the seat he began to talk. "Been studying Eskimo culture – living with them," he said, "learned their language. Got to know them well enough so they took me whaling with them. Soon

I realized that to understand their culture, I had to understand Eskimo whaling. But one thing led to another, and once I got involved trying to understand their whaling, I realized I had to do that against the background and history of Yankee whaling. So, I started a study of the history of Yankee harvest of the bowhead whale – the favored whale of the Eskimo. I've been trying to reconstruct the entire history of that whaling." He shifted his long legs in the chair, feet pushing against a pile of my papers on the floor.

"Just was in Washington talking with the National Oceanographic and Atmospheric Administration. They said they'd fund my study if I could find a biologist who knew about counting animals and about endangered species. Several people recommended you. Get right to the point. I'm here to find out if you'd like to work with me on this project.

"We've got great historical records at the New Bedford Museum," Bockstoce said. He explained that most of the great Yankee whaling ships made New Bedford their headquarters. "The Yankee whaling ships left New Bedford in the fall, sailed south along the Atlantic coast of South America, around the Cape during its summer, then sailed north in the Pacific, stopped at Hawaii to refit and take on fresh water and food, and then headed north a year later to the Bering Straits to hunt bowhead.

"All the whaling voyages ever made are know, because newspapers of the day listed the departures and landings of every ship. And many of the logbooks from the bowhead whaling voyages still exist – we've got many at the Museum. Know where most of the others are around the country. My idea is to use the logbooks to reconstruct the entire history of the whaling – how many whales were killed, even estimate how many bowheads there used to be. That's why the NOAA people want me to find a biologist.

"So here I am," John said, wiping the dust from my office off his pantleg and picking up a few pieces of papers from the floor as he talked to me, putting them neatly on the laboratory counter next to him. "Would you like to work with me on this?" he asked.

We talked for several hours. John had an appealing skepticism and pleasing sense of humor. He had an honesty about what he did, about his experiences with the Eskimos, and with what he knew and did not know. It was a pleasant relief after my experiences with Richard Needles's tall tales about sperm whale acting like African gazelles. I expected that it would seem strange to my colleagues in ecology for me to start a project about bowhead whales with an anthropologist, but what the heck, I thought, I was working at Woods Hole studying elephants, I had done the one study about the social behavior of sperm whales which had turned into a total disaster. John's description of what we might accomplish was highly attractive to me. Perhaps we could use historical records to find out something we could never learn any other way – how many animals there had once been, and how their numbers had changed over time with the pressure of Yankee whaling.

"Sure," I said, liking John and the way he spoke about his work. He got up, muscles bulging from his shirt, put on his suitcoat, adjusted his suit pocket handkerchief and rimless glasses, shook hands and headed out the door. I watched out my window as he passed by outside, subject to strange side glances from Woods Hole scientists.

Thus, we began a strange cooperation: an anthropologist and an ecologist. John went around the country and located all the known existing logbooks. We began meeting regularly at Woods Hole, John always arriving in a three-piece suit looking as if he just stepped out of an advertisement for Brooks Brothers. Occasionally we would eat lunch at the Fishmonger where the expressions of the local scientists, seeing the elegantly dressed person, amused me. On one of these occasions John told me that he would be stopping work temporarily on our project because he had to undergo extensive dental repair. I asked him what the problem was.

"A few years ago, I spent about eighteen months in the Arctic, living with and studying the Eskimos, and generally traveling around on my own to explore old Eskimo sites," he said. "I was way out in the middle of nowhere, doing some studies of old Eskimo sites, and had to find my own food. Was out hunting for some carabao to eat, and I tripped on a patch of icy snow. Fell forward onto my rifle butt, knocked out all of my front teeth. Had to survive several months on my own that way, until I could get back to where there was transportation to the lower forty-eight." My opinion of John, already high, rose even more. This was no wimp, but a person who could survive alone, wounded, in the Arctic.

After his teeth were repaired, John began his regular visits again. One day when we took a break for lunch, he told me that he had just returned from London for another meeting of the International Whaling Commission. "Had a curious experience," he said, "Some guy tried to mug me, right in a nice part of the city, but I shook him off – got the police to take him," he said simply, and then turned to his lunch and to a discussion to whales.

Our first task was to secure funding for our study. We wrote a proposal, and I attended a meeting held by NOAA where I presented our ideas. Everything depended on the reaction of the other scientists at this meeting. I saw Richard Needles, the Canadian whale biologist who had led us astray with his tales of sperm whale behavior and my heart sunk. Here was a hostile audience. Then I spied Charley Russell, talking with his typical animation to a group of whale experts, dressed as usual in his casual once-white shirt open almost to his belly button. Before the meeting, he and I talked, and I told him about the plan for me to work with Bockstoce.

"Bockstoce?" He said, "He's amazing. Always dressed like a dandy, but don't underestimate him. He's one tough guy," said Charley. "You know, a few months ago I was standing at this bar in one of those gentlemen's clubs in London, one of those stuffy clubs, and there was this person standing next to me dressed in a three-piece suit. Only he was too young and too fit to be a member of the club. Decided he was a guest like me. We got talking and it was Bockstoce. He had a cut on his chin, and I asked him about it. He said that someone had just tried to mug him, but he had fought the attacker off. I bought him a drink and while we were standing there a policeman came in dragging this scruffy looking fellow who was moaning and whaling," Beddington continued.

"The policeman went over to Bockstoce and said 'Excuse me sir, but I believe you have broken this gentleman's jaw.' Very polite, the Bobbie was, and spoke very mildly, as if telling Bockstoce that he had just found him a better room or something. "Bockstoce explained to the Bobby that the man had tried to mug him."

So. I realized, this was the story Bockstoce had mentioned to me in an understated sentence.

"He had hauled off and socked the mugger one, then calmly came into the club and ordered a drink. One tough cookie," said Charlie, "calm as a clam, sipping his drink. `Broke this gentleman's jaw.' I'll tell you," Charlie laughed. "If you work with him, just don't get him angry. Might break your jaw too."

Since the 1970s, I have done cooperative research on bowhead whales with my excellent colleague and now close friend, John Bockstoce.

We used the logbooks from many Yankee Bowhead whaling ships. Each day the first mate would record the weather, the sea conditions, the sea ice conditions, and what whales and other marine mammals were seen, sought, and caught.

The data include more than 52,000 daily observations in an unbroken 65-year record from 1849 - 1914. Data was drawn from the logbooks and journals of the whaling industry representing 19% of all known whaling cruises made to those waters during the period. From these records we estimate that 18,650 whiles were killed and 16,600 were taken by the pelagic whaling industry, an average of about 280 whales killed and 250 whales taken per year. These estimates of the bowhead whale population for 1847 (the year before the beginning of exploitation by the whaling industry) suggested that the population numbered approximately 30,000, and was no less than 20,000 and no more than 40,000. The population appears to have been depleted rapidly: one-third of the total number of kills during the entire period of commercial whaling occurred in the first decade, and two-thirds of them in the first two decades. The ships' records also suggest that the species was rapidly eliminated from major parts of its range.

We were able to compare the southern edge of the north Pacific sea ice during our study period of the whaling ships, and found fascinating similarities between the ice age in spring and fall in those days with sea ice edges recording in the 1980s by Pacific moving ships. The scientific details are available on my website, www.danielbbotkin.com and also on the Bockstoce and Botkin Historical Sea Ice Data Study's home at the University of Alaska website.

The debate over our proposal was intense and mostly hostile until Russell, having listened carefully to the methods we were going to use, got up and spoke, as if a lightbulb had just gone off in his head. He said to the others that he just now understood what we were trying to do, and even though the method wasn't perfect, it was the only one that would work, and we would do an important thing and ought to be funded. He went on to describe how the International Whaling Commission could use our information. That organization, a voluntary one of nations involved in whaling or interested in whaling, set catch limits for each species of whale. Charlie explained that if we could find out how many bowheads there used to be, we might be able to help set a realistic limit on the allowed catch by the Eskimos. Russell carried the day and won the argument on our behalf. I tried to thank him, but he brushed it off and headed into town to find a bar and see if there were any good-looking women about.

Soon after, Bockstoce and I began our work in earnest. John collected logbooks from twenty percent of the voyages ever made. In those logbooks, the first mate wrote each day at noon a report about the previous and present day's activities. He wrote down the ship's location in latitude and longitude, sea conditions, the visibility in miles, and the percent of the ocean covered by ice, if any. He had a stamp in the shape of a whale and stamped that whale picture in the logbook margin every time a whale was caught. There was a blank in the center of the whale stamp and the first mate wrote within it the number of barrels of oil obtained from each whale. That number told us an approximate size of a whale.

We hired six people who spent six months typing into a computer the first mate's daily observations from all the days of all the logbooks Bockstoce had gathered. Then we began our analysis. We divided the northern Pacific Ocean into latitude and longitude zones, from Canada and Alaska to Siberia, and north into the Bering Straits and above in the waters north of Canada. With the computer, we were able to create maps that showed the numbers of bowheads caught in each part of the Pacific and the Bering Sea during each decade during the entire Yankee Whaling period, which lasted from 1840 until the first World War.

In the early years of the whaling, many were caught in the southern part of the bowhead's range – about halfway between Hawaii and the Bering Straits. But these whales were rapidly depleted, and the catch moved northward, decade by decade.

We learned from these maps that a third of all the bowheads ever caught by the Yankee whalers were caught in the first decade, from 1840 to 1850, and two-thirds in the first twenty years. During all the remaining time the ships left New Bedford for the arduous voyage around the Cape and north, from 1860 to 1920, sixty years, only a final third were caught. The catch declined rapidly, but even so the whaling ships continued to search for bowheads.

By the end of the era, voyages took three years. Ships sailed north of the Bering Straits, overwintered locked in the ice, and then hunted the whales when the waters opened and the whales returned. Often a group of whaling ships would anchor nearby each other. A painting made by a member of one of these ships' crews shows men playing baseball and soccer on the ice in well laid out playing fields. cleared of snow with whaling ships locked in the ice around them.

Officers sometimes brought their wives on the voyages, and food was plentiful from the sea. Impressive banquets were held, for which a whaling ship would print formal invitations. One of these that still exists shows an elaborate menu of shellfish and fin fish that would delight many a table today, and would be a rare treat, considering the over-fishing of most of the species listed on the menu that has taken place since.

Every year at Woods Hole there was the Black Dog Contest, a kind of carnival that celebrated the intentionally casual character and dress of this research village. It was held on a large open green behind the Marine Biological Laboratory, and featured high school students preforming short plays, local scientists who had such hobbies as circus acrobatics, a man dressed as a clown who danced with a life-sized floppy, three-legged doll, various things to eat, and the central feature, the black dog contest. Entries could be black dogs, but other kinds were accepted, including people dressed up as black dogs, people not dressed as black dogs, and anything else that someone thought was amusing.

I was wandering around the Black Dog Contest grounds, observing this celebration of the new casualness, when Bockstoce turned up in a dark blue three-piece suit and matching tie. He said he was somewhat in a hurry but had just come back from the annual meeting of the International Whaling Commission in Cambridge England.

"You might think this stuff about bowhead whales and their catch is nothing – not important, but that's not how it's seen at the IWC," he said. "During the meeting, the Japanese delegation proposed an increase in their take of whales on the grounds that this was a traditional cultural practice. The American delegation opposed it, on the grounds that no hunting of an endangered species was right. An Eskimo poured red ink all over one of the Japanese representatives, and there was a danger of a fight," he said. "Then I overheard one of the Canadian delegates speaking to one of our Americans reps. He said `What are you going to do about your indigenous cultural problem?' and the American looked confused. `What cultural problem?' he said. `Well, you just argued against the Japanese taking whales for cultural reasons, but you've got a treaty with the Eskimo that gives them the right to take whales. So, you're contradicting yourself.'"

"This made our study pretty important," continued Bockstoce, glancing at the current entry in the black dog contest, a thin girl in black tights. "Suddenly, the Americans realized they had to negotiate an allowed harvest by the Eskimo and needed to know how many that might be without harming the species. Someone mentioned our study, and now they want to know our results – how many bowheads had there been? They can use this to estimate how many might be taken."

We were standing and watching the clown dance with the three-legged floppy rag doll, to which Bockstoce made no comment. He shook my hand and hurried off, much to the amazement of the rest of the crowd that included many Harvard and Radcliff students doing their best to look scruffy, most wearing fairly new blue jeans and looking somewhat uncomfortable. Here and there I could spot a student from New York City, because New Yorkers knew how to be scruffy and there they were, in dirty T-shirts, worn jeans, and basketball sneakers starting to come apart at the seams, looking quite at home, but giving Bockstoce a strange look. So, I thought, here is a chance that we might finally make a difference in a real-world situation, actually help save an endangered species, and it was because for once we had good data – we were finally able to answer one of the simple questions that kept coming up in my work, this one simply: how many bowhead whales ever lived on the Earth? And the key to it was, from the point of view of most of the other Woods Hole professionals, a commonly odd-ball and out of place person who dressed all wrong.

I saw Erene walking around the Black Dog contest by herself, so I introduced her to Bockstoce and asked her to join us. I was with the two best dress people in Woods Hole, I thought. John took his leave and Erene and I continued to walk and watch the other Woods Hole inhabitants, in the contest and outside. She invited me and my two children for dinner that evening at her house.

Our work took several years, and the method for estimating the original abundance of bowheads was not one of the strongest statistically. But it was the best we could do. In the end, our data indicated that there had been about twenty thousand bowheads at the start of the Yankee whaling era in 1840, give or take ten thousand – somewhere between ten thousand and thirty thousand whales. At the time the Black Dogs were contesting, there were about 6,000 bowheads swimming in the Pacific.

The International Whaling Commission used our estimate of the original abundance and compared it with the present. Their rationale was that the pre-Yankee harvesting number of bowheads was the natural number and an abundance that should have remained constant year after year as long as there was no interference from Europeans and Americans with their modern technologies. This led, through a series of political negotiations at the International Whaling Commission meetings, to a reduction in the allowed take by the Eskimos of one bowhead per year, a small change since they were allowed previously to catch 40.

Well, I had succeeded in finding out the answer to some question, and even more, a question about how many animals of a species there once were. Finally, a success. But the effect on the conservation of endangered species was saving one whale a year. Not a world-shattering victory, I pondered as I made yet another attempt to clean up my office and put the papers from the bowhead study into some kind of order.

And the assumption of the IWC that there had been a natural number of bowheads that was unchanging, and it was natural just because no Yankee hunted them, wore at me. I just could not accept it. The abundances of all animals had to vary with climatic change, changes in ocean currents, ups and downs of the production of food that an animal ate. Thinking it over, I decided that there was a much more straightforward approach. If there were six thousand bowheads now, and if we could give some kind of estimate of their reproductive rate, we could figure out how many whales might be harvested without damaging the population. One percent of 6,000 is sixty, and the IWC and the U S Government treaty with the Eskimos was allowing a take of less than forty. Since the reproductive rate of large mammals was low, but not as low as one percent, this seemed to be a rather safe level of harvest, and much less than the hundreds of bowhead that had been taken in some of the early years of the Yankee whaling of the bowhead. The victory seemed less and less the more I thought about it.

But we had at least reconstructed a fascinating history of one of the world's great creatures, and we had created a set of maps like a moving picture show of how the bowheads had been hunted and how they had retreated northward, always northward, against the onslaught of the Yankee fishermen. Only the combination of what Bockstoce knew as an anthropologist and the kind of thing I knew about populations could have led to that reconstruction. We had not saved the world, but we had done a small thing that was unique. We had found a way to count a population long dead, and to track its changes over time, through written history. Finally, we had answered a seemingly simple question: How many bowhead whales used to swim the oceans?"

Bockstoce and I have continued our cooperative research ever since, cooperating as well with the whale researchers in Alaska whom he had known for years, and in the decades since are using highly sophisticated equipment to study the whales. When concern built up about climate change— the warming of Earth's surface temperature in some of the 20th century, we realized that many of the whaling ship logbooks had detailed information about the location of the Pacific Arctic ice age. This is because the bowhead whales tended to feed at the southern ice edge. This is where the ocean waters have an upwelling—rising currents that bring nutrients and many small creatures to the surface, which the bowheads liked to eat. This meant that the many logbook daily entries had information about where the southern edge of the ice was between 1840 and the first decade of the 20th Century. We abstracted those data, created maps showing where the ice edge was by season over that time. It turned out that the ice edge in the northern Pacific during that Yankee bowhead whaling time was close to the ice edge locations in the 1980s.

And I had come to know one of the most fascinating characters I had ever met, one who has been a lifelong friend and I have respected all my entire life.

CHAPTER 26

Politeness Under Gunfire

Shots rang out and I could hear bullets rattling around in the branches of the beech tree just above my head. I was on the eastern edge of Hutcheson Memorial Forest, the last remaining uncut forest in the state of New Jersey, taking a few people on a nature walk through the woods, part of my job as caretaker. It was a warm fall afternoon, one of those Indian summer October days that seem to be summer stretched out to dry. Some leaves were turning color but many were still green. There was a musty scent from the fallen leaves on the ground, and the blue sky had a few hazy clouds.

I had come across people with guns in this no-trespassing, no-hunting preserve. Part of my job was to patrol it and keep it a preserve, undisturbed by trespassers. But I had never actually been shot at. My initial reaction wasn't fear; it was anger. I was just plain mad that anybody would be shooting into this last stand of virgin forests, especially with me in the line of fire. Taking cover behind the tree, I waited for some more shots to see where the gunfire was coming from. The next volley made it clear that someone was shooting from the land next to the forest, just east, where there was a private house. I guided the guests quickly away from the line of fire and took them back to the visitors' parking area. I made sure they were safely on their way and then got on the phone and called Murray Buell, the director of the nature pre-serve and my major professor.

Murray, a great naturalist, was also a skillful fund-raiser and spokes-person for nature. For years, he had studied this small uncut woodlot near Rutgers University, where he was on the faculty. The 65-acre woodlot had been owned since 1701 by one family, the Mettlers, the original Dutch settlers. A few years before my arrival at Rutgers, the Mettlers had decided to sell the woods and Murray had succeeded in raising funds to purchase it as a nature preserve for the university. He had raised money from Sinclair Oil and the carpenters' union, among other sources, and agreed to name the woods after one of the heads of the union, Hutcheson.

Murray had persuaded the carpenters' union that the woods needed watching and therefore needed a live-in supervisor, and that the car-penters should build a house for this caretaker. They did, and Murray turned the caretaker's job into a scholarship for a graduate student. I was fortunate to obtain that scholarship, and my young family with my two toddler kids was able to live near the beautiful forest, with a stream running out from it down near the house. I gave nature tours on week-ends and patrolled the woods frequently, preventing people as much as I could from removing plants and shooting deer in the forest.

Not too many days before the shots rattled over my head, I had confronted a hunter illegally dragging a deer out of Hutcheson forest across one of the research areas-a series of previously farmed fields that were growing back to forest, and were in use in experiments as com-parisons with the ancient forest.

The hunter dragged his deer right through somebody's study plots, damaging the plants and roughing up the soil. I had hurried out of the caretaker's house and dashed into the field, standing between the hunter and the highway, a hundred yards or so behind me, where he was heading. Hands on my hips, I lectured him about the rules as he was dragging his still bleeding and therefore poorly cared for carcass right through a research area. It was an unequal argument.

"Says who?" the hunter asked, casually shifting his rifle that he had crooked under one arm so that its barrel pointed at me. I didn't think that he wasn't going to give up his deer to a young unarmed graduate student when nobody else was in sight. He dragged his deer right by me. That wasn't my first confrontation with hunters and trespassers. One of my predecessors had himself deputized and carried a gun, but I did not want to take that approach Most of them thought there wasn't much point patrolling without a weapon.

Sometimes I was overzealous about this. The previous spring, I had come across an elderly and kindly gentleman who came into the forest land with a small spade. He spoke with a thick Italian accent. He told me that he had been coming to these woods for years, most of the years since he had emigrated from Italy to harvest mushrooms, and didn't know that it had become a nature preserve or that he was doing anything illegal. I shooed him off as was my duty, but all my friends thought I had just been mean to the old gentleman, and what were a few mushrooms to the ancient forest?

These experiences rushed through my mind as I hurried into the caretaker's office and called my professor, Murray Buell. I thought he would not be at work, although he and his botanist wife, Helen, often worked through the weekends in their laboratory. "Murray, there's a man shooting into the forest and he just shot over my head" I shouted into the phone. "It's that neighbor---the one who doesn't like the fact that the woods is no longer as open to the public as it used to be. You've got to come right away and talk with him." Since Murray was the director, he should confront the neighbor, I thought. "It's that neighbor---the one who doesn't like the fact that the woods is no longer as open to the public as it used to be. You've got to come right away and talk with him."

Murray agreed and drove out immediately. He asked to see where the bullets had fallen, and I took him into the forest to the beech tree and told him the story. The neighbor's house was just visible through the trees and there was a man out there with a pistol.

Murray walked back to the house saying little. He motioned to me that I should get into his car and we would visit the house next door. Murray was a native of Shelbourne, Massachusetts, and was a New England gentleman of the finest sort, always soft-spoken, always polite, never directly confrontational. He was not a wallflower and did not shy away from controversies, but he handled them always in his quiet and polite New England manner. He was like my father-in-law Heman Chase in this way.

Heman and his wife, Edith, however, often joked about New England customs, one of which was that a family never used the parlor, their formal living room, except for weddings and funerals and other major events, perhaps a visit from the governor, if that ever happened. Instead, the rural New England custom was to enter the house through the kitchen door. It was considered uppity to appear at the front door that went through the parlor unless one was specifically asked to do so.

Heman and Edith wanted people to enter at the front door of the house they had built themselves and had purposely built their house so that the front door faced directly onto their long gravel driveway.

There was no gravel or stone path around to the kitchen door, which could be reached only by walking clear around the house on the lawn and climbing a set of wooden stairs to the back porch. They had hoped that this would discourage the traditional practice, but it did not. They laughed when they told me how many people made that long trek, not willing to risk being impolite from the traditional New England point of view.

But this was not on my mind after the pistol shots had rattled around the tree limbs above me. Murray drove slowly out the forest driveway and into the neighbor's, dawdling along as if he were thinking carefully what to do. "Come on, Murray," I said. "We've got to catch the guy with his gun out." I was still furious. But Murray wasn't about to be hurried. He parked at the front of the house and sat there in silence for a few min- utes while I waited i patiently. I wanted to run to the front door and bang at it loudly.

When Murray climbed out of the car, he walked slowly past the front door, around the side of the house into the backyard, where by this time there was nobody holding a gun. He climbed the steps to the back door and rapped lightly on the kitchen door. "For God's sake, Murray, this is no time to be polite," I said, too agitated to stay within the proper submissive graduate student role.

But Murray said nothing. He was not going to violate the correct New England behavior he had grown up with, no matter what the cause. Eventually, the man of the house appeared at the door, and Mur-ray spoke with him in a low voice. At first, the man denied any knowledge of a gun or shooting, but Murray prevailed. Finally, he ad-mitted that he had been target practicing, but he claimed he had been shooting at a target in his backyard that was now put away. To hit the beech tree that I had stood under while trying to shoot at a target where he pointed would have meant that his aim was off about 60 degrees. Stories had circulated that this neighbor used to shoot birds in Mettler's woods for sport. I'm sure that was what he was doing, but we had arrived too late, because of Murray's cultural captivity, to catch the liar in action with his gun.

After a half hour's mild confrontation, we left, and Murray suggested we let it go. "He'll think twice now about shooting into the woods," he said. "I hope he'll think more times than that," I said, wishing that the old New England customs were a little more flexible and more aggressive. I did not believe we had dissuaded the gunslinger at all, and I continued to wish that Murray had banged on the front door, called the police, and had the guy arrested. But the tradition of politeness, even in dealing with random acts of violence potentially dangerous to one of his graduate students, was not to take precedence over Murray's upbringing.

So it is with much that happens to us with nature. We are trapped by our culture to seek the back door into understanding the life around us, even when that may be the most inappropriate and ineffectual path to a solution.

CHAPTER 27

My Uncle Harry And My Wife,
Diana. Talent As A Gift.

In 1912, my Uncle Harry left his home in Boston when he was 16 and
he to New York, alone, to become a commercial artist. He was a great
success. Within ten years he had made so much money that he was able
to stop working travel to Paris and live there for ten years, where he
studied fine art. Uncle Harry was born right-handed, but contracted
polio which paralyzed his right arm. As a child he had to teach himself
to draw and paint left-handed, which he did with great success. After
ten years in Paris, Uncle Harry returned to New York City, and lived
in a small apartment on 4th Street in Greenwich Village until his death
in 1988, spending the summers at Provincetown, Cape Cod, a popular
artist colony during that time.

Uncle Harry was a small person, about 5'2" but he had an imposing
personality, enhanced by black hair and a black goatee, which he cul-
tivated to take his audience's eyes away from his withered arm, which
he never exposed in public and I never saw. His right hand was always
in his sport coat pocket, and he managed never to expose it, however,
itchy or sweaty it may have become. I say "his audience" because Uncle

Harry was always on stage, a performer, an actor, a personality, a presence, even if it were just him and me sitting in the living room.

I loved fine paintings and going to major museums to view them, even though I couldn't draw anything that looked realistic. I had absolutely no talent as a graphic artist. All the more reason I was fascinated by great art.

I was always impressed by Uncle Harry from the time of my first recollections. Then he seemed a tall person in my eyes, who came into our living room and began to order his younger brother, my father, around, and tell my father what, exactly, he was doing wrong and how he should correct it. My father, Benjamin, a gentle person to the outside world but a tyrant to his family, was cowed by his brother, and this indeed impressed me deeply. I was in awe of this person with a black goatee who painted pictures that hung in famous art galleries. Having an artist in the family was a fascination, and for years I wanted to ask Uncle Harry about painting. Why did he do it? How did he get ideas? What was the meaning of his pictures, which were by this time in his life completely abstract? But as a child, I didn't have the courage to speak to this impressive artist.

Finally, when I was home from college and was about 19, I got up my courage. Uncle Harry and his second wife, Rhoda, had come out of New York City for Thanksgiving, as they usually did. When we met him at the train, Uncle Harry descended with the aristocratic air of one doing us a favor, who had deemed it necessary for us that he make this expedition from the center of life to the edge of civilization, Croton-on-Hudson, New York, 30 miles upriver from Greenwich Village. Rhoda, a pretty pale blond with stylish high cheekbones, trailed quietly in the back. We ushered them home and, after Uncle Harry had berated his brother for the sins of the past year and we had eaten my mother's huge turkey dinner, we sat in the living room. Only Uncle Harry, Rhoda and I were there, and there was an awkward silence.

"Uncle Harry," I said, gathering all my will power, suppressed for 19 years of experiencing this imperial presence. "Eh, I've always wanted to ask you about art — about your art. . . " I hesitated.

Suddenly, the dam broke, Uncle Harry relaxed, "I love to talk about my art," he said.

"Well, Uncle Harry, when I go to the Museum of Modern Art and look at the abstract paintings, I can see a meaning in them sometimes, but I wonder whether the artist had a meaning in mind — had that same meaning I had in his mind," I said.

"That's a good question," Uncle Harry said, "Now in my case, I make it a point that my paintings *do not* have a meaning — they are symbolism, they are art. If you find a meaning in one of them, that's fine with me, but it is your meaning, not mine. I make a conscientious effort to paint what is artistic — to paint beauty, design. Now there are other painters who do see their paintings as messages, as symbolism, but not me and there are many others like me."

Uncle Harry was clearly amazed. This unimportant, uncommunicative son of his younger brother actually thought about art and had something intelligent to ask. It didn't hurt that it was about his own paintings and his own process of paintings. We spent the afternoon in a wonderful philosophical discussion about art, and when Uncle Harry and Rhoda headed out the door to the train, he said to my father, "It's so nice to know that you have a son with an interest in art."

From that day on, Uncle Harry and I always had something interesting to talk about. One day he told me about how he got started.@@

"Uncle Harry, how did you do it — how did you leave home at 16 and become a successful commercial artist in New York," I asked. It was truly bewildering to me, who at 20 couldn't image projecting myself into a success on any stage to speak of *The City*.

"Of course, I did have one advantage. I was able to live at the home of my cousins, George and Ira Gershwin, and they encouraged me as well."

"Well, when I started, I was nobody, so I had to make a good impression," Uncle Harry said. "I would get an interview and would go to show my portfolio. When I left my apartment, I would find somebody on the street looking to make a little money, and I would hire him for a few hours. I gave him my portfolio and told him where and when to bring it. Then I would go to the interview with nothing in my hand and tell the editor of a magazine who was interviewing me that my assistant would be along shortly with my drawings. That's how I got started."

"You know, although I do abstract painting today, I pride myself on the fact that when I was a commercial artist I could draw so things looked completely real — some artists do abstract art because they *can't* draw," Uncle Harry said one day.

"What kinds of things did you draw?" I asked.

"In those days, there was no color photography, so all color advertisements were drawn by artists like me," Uncle Harry said. "I could paint anything," he continued. "Why you know I could do a painting of a glass of wine with the drops of water condensing on the outside, so real that you would think you could touch those drops," he said.

I was fascinated by that possibility, all the more so because I had never been able to draw anything. The image of a painting so real of a glass of wine that you could almost touch the water condensing on the glass stayed with me, reappeared to me, continued as kind of Socratic ideal of the perfection of art. It tantalized me. How could you do this. Finally, six years later, when I was 26 and working in New York City for the first time, as an scientific journalist for the *World Wide Medical News Service*, my first professional job as a journalist, and my first real job at anything, I had an evening at home and little money to spend, and a young daughter and wife, who was also an artist and had oil paints. I borrowed her paints and a small canvas. We had no wine in the apartment, so I filled a wine glass with red wine vinegar and, by the most careful process of deconstruction and analysis, by a qualitative trig-onometry, by staring at the wine glass to see exactly what colors there were in the reflections on a glass surface (white), I was able to paint a wine glass that looked real, and on which the painted drops of water looked as if they might be touched. It was clearly not the work of a professional, but I have proved to myself that my Uncle Harry's tech-nique was repeatable. Thank you, Uncle Harry.

"One thing that amazes me about the great, realistic painters," I said to Uncle Harry one day, "is how, sometimes in the background there will be a horse and rider, or a person walking along carrying a burden, and it looks completely real, but when you go close up and examine it, there are just four or five quick brush strokes." I said. "How do they — and you — do that?" I asked.

"Hmmm, I never thought about it," was his only answer. My God, I thought. Here am I, unable to draw anything that looks more than a child's attempt. And here was my Uncle, whose artistic talent was so great, so intrinsic, that he never had to even think about it. He could just do it.

In my life I have come across this level of talent with other people. The most striking in addition to Uncle Harry's ability to paint many styles of art, was the talent of my wife, Diana Gerjoy (Perez, Botkin). She told me that ever since she was four years old, she could hear a song sung and immediately go to a piano and play it exactly, with two hands, with all the harmony and melodies. This talent grew with her as she matured, and today and for many decades past, she could not only play any melody with exactly the right chords, but also with the exact style and feeling of the original. At various places she and I have visited, the owners discovered this amazing talent, and she would end up sitting at a piano while an audience—it could be from one family to an entire invited group --- called out favorite songs from their life, any kind, any style. And she would play it immediately, perfectly, again with all the chords and melodies, harmony ---- exactly the correct chords — and exactly the mood, the feeling, the style of the original that she had heard some time often long before exactly as it way. In the original.

Sometimes, we have hired a young person as Diana and I have matured, and each one would say "Diana, you've got to play some current songs." She smiled and agreed, so the young woman would take out her iPhone and get some currently fashionable pop song that was one of her favorites, and Diana, hearing it just once, would play it exactly, with the current modern style, rhythm, chording, all the things that were in the original. Her listener would smile and exclaim as to how exactly her rendition was.

Her musical talent went beyond that. After we were married, I began to work with a professional music/video producer, Sergio Cavalieri (whom I told about in an earlier chapter). He told me he had been trained in classical music, explained to me why Bach had to be the greatest of all Western Civilization's classical music composers. He also play electric guitar in a Rock and Roll band in his native Brazil, which had sold a huge number of albums, I don't even remember the number but I think it reached in the millions.

I met Sergio when I decided to make a CD of myself singing folk songs and first telling the story of the origin of each. I had done this my whole life, making my first record when I was 6 years old, and had decided I should leave a memory of this behind for my children. Half way through the recording, I took a break, and Sergio said there was a lot in what I had done, including the singing, the guitar, and the entire style, along with the story of the song's history. He urged me to go on with it, and together we joined and formed a company called "What Makes Us One," because, as I explained to Sergio, in American history whenever a very tough time happened, Americans turned to folk songs for emotional relief, include some then famous protest songs. I said the change in our time was that we had a very tough time as a society, but people had mostly forgotten folk music.

We started recording, Sergio and I, but then I suggested that we had to get some very young musicians from some musical approach but not familiar to folk music to come and listened while I played and sang them an old time folk song, or played them an old 78 rpm record of an American or British folk song, of many styles, and then told each "Do it your way." The results were wonderful. We loved the different take on the old song, often greatly improving it, at least for our modern tastes. One of the best was a Chilean woman trained in opera singing.

I listened to her once and thought she was the perfect person to sing and record a Scottish folksong I had learned from my Junior year in college spent at the University of Edinburgh, where I got very involved in Scottish and English folk songs.

One of these songs went through my head often, but especially if I was feeling a bit down and out for a long walk. It would just come to me and I would either just listen to it mentally, or actually sing it. It was "Died for Love," the lyrics are below. She sang it so beautifully that whenever I give a talk about folk music and played some samples, as soon as her recording comes on, the audience always said "I could listen to her all day."

Died for Love
(Traditional Scottish folk song)

A bold young farmer courted me
He gained my love and my liberty
He gained my love with such good will
And I have to admit that I love him still

I wish, I wish, my but it's all in vain,
I wish I was a maid again,
But a maid again I never shall be,
Because a young farmer lay still with me.

I wish my baby little was born
And smileth on his father's knee
And I poor girl was dead and gone
And the green grass grew all over me.

Go dig my grave both wide and deep
Put a marble stone at my head and feet

And above it all put a turtle white dove
To show to the world that I died for love.

Now there was talent. But my wife's Diana's talent went even be-yond. Sergio and I would make a tape of a folk song, me introducing it to him as I sang it and played the guitar. He would then, with much greater skill and musical talent, add an electric guitar co-melody, and then would get other musician friends to add drums and whatever other instruments seemed appropriate. It was great fun.

But both of us being cautious, I would ask Diana to come to the studio and listen to the latest recording we had made. She would sit in silence listening. But one of the first times she did this, during the play-back of the recording, she stood up and said "Stop" to Sergio, who halted the playback. "The top note of that last chord is wrong," Diana said. I didn't think I was a bad musician, but this ability went beyond anything I had ever heard, including many times some of the best folk musicians would come to our home and get recorded, or I would listen to them in England, Scotland, and recordings from around the world. But Diana's standing up and telling Sergio to stop, that top note of the last chord was wrong, went completely beyond me. I heard a chord alright, but I couldn't say its top note was wrong—I thought it all sounded good. Such things always sounded good to me.

Diana and Sergio would then have a discussion. Sometimes he would reply to her that that was a jazz chord, and she just wasn't used to it. They would argue and half the time Sergio would give in and tell Diana she was right and he changed that chord.

There again was an innate talent that like my Uncle Harry's ability to paint a beautiful painting in many different styles. My wife, Diana had a similarly amazing natural talent in music.

I had studied music theory at the University of Rochester Eastman School of Music where I took clarinet lessons (I also play classical music (and with other naturally highly talented musicians near to but not at Diana's level. During college days, I wanted to learn how to play more kinds of popular music, so I got in touch with a family friend who was a piano tuner and played music in various restaurants and bars. He taught me music theory, including much about how all the chords played on a piano were connected, and the names of various complexes of chords.

One day years later, Diana and I were playing and singing together. We had picked a very nice old folk song with unusual chording. Diana immediately played it exactly as I sang it and played on the guitar. But then she started adding wonderful chords that fit beautifully with the melody. I stopped her and said "Diana, that was a beautiful C minor sixth chord you just played, and it is perfect for that point in that song."

"Thank you," she said, "But what's a C minor sixth chord?"

Just like Uncle Harry. Same kind of answer. Music was so natural, so innate with her as painting was for Uncle Harry that she didn't have to know any of the theory, it was all just there.

Well, I keep playing folk music, but when it comes time to pick a chord for a particular point in a song, she plays me what it should be. I would ask her what the chord was called, but she never knew, so I had to go look at her fingers to see what notes she was playing.

Some of us are born so lucky that we have a talent that we never have to explain, think about, but just do it. That was my Uncle Harry and is my wife Diana. That's not my level certainly with painting and only pretty good with music. Yes, some people are born with gifts that come from who knows where and make life, which is often difficult, wonderful. Thank God!

Thoreau's Transit

[The new settlers of Pennsylvania take] little account of Natural History, that science being here (as in other parts of the world) looked upon as a mere trifle, and the pastime of fools. Peter Kalm, European traveler and writer about the new American nation *(Travels Into North America) (1750)5*

In the mid-1990s, I was canoeing in Maine with several companions, following the routes of Henry David Thoreau more than a century before us. Our plan was to make a film about Thoreau and nature, and I was also going to write a book to go along with the film. It was early in the morning and we had just put our canoes into Oyster Pond on the west branch of the Penobscot River, several hours drive from Millinocket, Maine, beginning a two-day journey. We canoed round the first bend, just out of sight of our put-in point, when we surprised a cow moose, or she surprised us, and she moved quickly from the center of the stream up onto the bank, then turned and looked at us, water dripped from her drooping, bearded jaw as she chewed on a stem of a water plant she had pulled from the bottom of the stream.

Although it was cloudy and beginning to drizzle, Ted Timreck, a professional film maker who had proposed the idea for the book and film about Thoreau, pulled his movie camera from its watertight case and began filming, standing up in his canoe. Lori Barg, a graduate student and an experienced forester we had hired to help paddle, was in the back of Ted's canoe, and she quickly rowed to shore. Ted jumped out and followed the cow moose as she alternately moved off slowly and stopped and looked at us somewhat alarmed and possibly threateningly. Several times she pulled at a few leaves of a blueberry bush and seemed to calm slightly.

In another canoe, I sat and watched the goings-on with Parker Huber, our mentor and guide on the trip. Parker had walked and canoed every mile that Thoreau had traveled in the Maine Woods. He had done this several times and written a wonderful book about it, a guide to Thoreau's travels with maps and photographs, titled *The Wildest Country*. He was a devotee of Thoreau and sought the same kinds of things from nature that Thoreau had sought more than a century before. Tall and lanky, Parker was comfortable with the outdoors and an excellent canoeist and companion. We became fast friends and talked about how Thoreau approached the study of nature and how he made contact with nature.

Journals of explorers and the first naturalists to travel in America have fascinated me since the 1970s, when I was dodging bullets with Murray Buell in Hutcheson Memorial Forest, discussing economic principles with Heman Chase as we repaired the old mill and surveyed New Hampshire's woods, and when I was trying to find out how much water an elephant drank and how long a whale slept. Ted had suggested a book about Thoreau. Part of the reason I had readily agreed to the idea was my fascination with the way the North America looked before it had been changed by western civilization, and to rediscover that country now. But also, after several decades trying to help solve environmental problems, I had to admit that I was curious how Thoreau and other early naturalists and explorers approached the problems they encountered in nature. Maybe there were some lessons from the past. Perhaps they even had some keys that might help me find better ways to solve environmental problems today.

Our destination that day was an Inn located on a promontory of Moosehead lake called the *Chesuncook house*, reachable only by boat. The promontory had held a place for people to stay since Thoreau canoed this route in 1849. During his time, the location of the inn was the home of an Ansel Smith who had cleared about 100 acres, grew hay, and put up lumbermen and other travelers in the Maine woods. It was, interestingly, the last building that Thoreau described on that trip in the Maine Woods before he returned to civilization. Thoreau had canoed this route primarily to see and hunt moose with his Indian guide – he wanted to understand the entire Indian hunting process.[6] So our find of a moose was fortunate not only for Ted's filming, but also for our desire for verisimilitude.

While we watched Tim following the moose, Parker and I talked about Thoreau. The sky was cloudy, and a light drizzle fell, but it was a warm summer day, so we stretched out and chatted, ignoring the rain.

"Something that interested me about Thoreau's writing about the Maine woods, and I wanted to talk with you about" I said to Parker, " is although he tells you a lot about the woods, he also spends a lot of time talking about what his Indian guide is doing and the skills of the Indian guide, which he has a lot of admiration for, and talking about the sense of being in the place, which is different than just describing the countryside. He gives you his own feel for it."[7]

"Yes, yes. Absolutely," said Parker. "He was very enamored of the Indians, wanted to learn their ways. And I think he really gives us a genuine picture of the Indian, not romanticized -- all the sides he saw of them. And there's another quality, too in Thoreau's writings. It seems to me he's able to really be present in the moment, which I think you were talking about. The experience itself is something he strives for as much as he can —--with all his senses."

All his senses. An interesting thought. I mused about it while Ted climbed back in his canoe and Lori paddled them out from shore. The drizzle had let up so Ted kept his camera out and ready. He was grinning broadly; we had thought we might have had a chance to see a moose, but not within five minutes of putting in our canoes.

We continued down the west branch of the Penobscot River, passing some mild white water which took our attention, but then the Penobscot smoothed out for a while, and Parker spoke up again.

"Being here. Doing this. Canoeing. I think it gives us, in addition to all the spiritual refreshment that we receive out here, it gives us, I think, the same kind of fulfillment it gave Henry," Parker said. "And the same kind of discovery of yourself, as well as the natural world. It was kind of the inner and outer world with him, and the two were being worked on at the same time, I think in his life. And each was helping to give insight to the other. So, I think just providing this kind of space to ourselves in our lives, it allows other things to enter, which we're not necessarily aware of or expecting. And Thoreau could be very open to that kind of travel."

Spiritual refreshment. Discovery of yourself. An inner and outer world. Open to that kind of travel. Indeed, Thoreau was all of that. He had spent the last ten years of his life mainly in his home town of Concord, Massachusetts, taking a four hour walks every day to study the trees and flowers, birds and small mammals, to see how things changed with the seasons, and to find for himself the spiritual feelings of the outdoors.

Ted spoke up as he and Lori passed us in their canoe.

"That's an interesting theme," he said. "What are the accidents that happen when you're traveling and how does that relate to your traveling and Thoreau's?"

"I think you're traveling for the unexpected, and to just be here," Parker replied. "You don't really have to go anywhere. Matter of fact, we could just camp some place and wait for it to happen, whatever that might be. You wouldn't really know what it would be, but something would happen, and we would certainly have a further understanding of ourselves in the natural world. It takes a great deal of patience to be a naturalist."

Another intriguing thought. Don't have to go anywhere. Can experience nature right where you are. As the spruce and fir passed us up the slope from the Penobscot, I thought about that idea. "You don't really have to go anywhere." Thoreau had said it succinctly in one of his famous phrases. "I have traveled widely in Concord." He had also traveled extensively through the Maine woods, a wild country in his day, as parts of it are so in ours. But he discovered he did not need to travel far to discover himself or to discover nature. A patient naturalist. Not exactly a description of myself, but it did seem to fit Parker.

We passed a clearing in the woods, filled with blueberries and huckleberries.

"Do you feel you've been changed yourself by following his travels?" I asked Parker, "I mean, you've been everywhere he's every been and you been there several times."

"Well, that's a good question. I guess I ask myself each time I come back, what would I bring back from an experience like this," Parker replied. "What would I try to incorporate into my life at home from this, is the question. And I don't always have an answer for that, but somehow there's a fulfillment that stays within me that helps to center me in the daily world, and so I'm able to retain that for a while. And by coming back, or the memory of it, to rejuvenate that feeling again, within."

Incorporate the experience into my life at home. A fulfillment that stays with you. Helps center you in the daily world. Rejuvenation. It was the connection between the Maine woods and life at home that mattered to Parker, not the woods for themselves only. Searching for rejuvenation.

"There's something to do with the pace that we're moving. Out here, we're moving ourselves naturally, with our own rhythm, so you come to see what that's like, and at times it's possible to repeat that rhythm in your daily life -- it's coming back to solitude, to stillness, simplicity, silence, all these."

"So you can bring back a different sense of yourself because you've experienced that solitude and space and stillness. Silence was a great teacher for Thoreau, and his walks he preferred to be alone —-- because that was where a lot of insight came, in the silent spaces. But in Maine, here, where he was with the Indians, they're kind of guiding him into the natural world."

We grew silent ourselves and turned to paddling. It had been a magic moment, on the Penobscot River in the drizzling rain, immersed in nature's water and woods, listening to Parker talk about the reasons he kept coming back here. We passed a clearing in the woods, then pass by once again a dense forest of spruce, fir, and occasional birch. A bird flew above the trees, passing too quickly for us to identify it. Ducks swam on the river, keeping ahead of us, flying low over the water if we approached too close, then settling back down on the Penobscot, to float patiently, waiting for us.

We came to a place on the shore where most of the trees were dead and standing. This caught our curiosity, so we pulled our canoes out and looked over this patch of forest. We couldn't tell from our brief visit was had caused the dieback – maybe an insect outbreak or a flooding of the stream. But the forest was regenerating, with small spruce and fir growing under the dead trees, undergoing the process of succession – the development of a forest – that Thoreau himself had written about, and a term that he was one of the first to use. It reminded me of Thoreau the scientist as well as, in our conversation of a while before, Thoreau the seeker, in search of nature and in search of himself. Two curious sides to the same person.

We canoed the entire day, traveling eighteen miles and reaching the *Chesuncook Lake House* in late afternoon, with plenty of time to set up our tents and get ready for dinner, cooked by a French chef who, along with his American wife, owned the Inn. I slept outside in my travel tent, so I could experience more this Maine woods at night. There was more pleasant rain during the night, beating lightly on my tent, making the tent feel all the cozier. The storm's winds blew on the lake in front of the Inn and I could hear the waters lapping at the shore. I opened the tent flap, put my head out and felt the rain and breezes on my face. All the senses. Center oneself in the daily world.

The next morning dawned bright and clear but with a stiff wind blowing straight onshore. Our plan was to canoe directly north across the lake and then up a channel to a takeout point. With the strong headwind, I was glad to have Parker in the back, the two of us canoeing together. We were buffeted by the bright waves, pushed back by the wind, warmed by the sun. All the senses.

Later in the fall, Parker, Ted, and I went to Cape Cod where we continued to follow in Thoreau's footsteps. We visited a house in Wellfleet where Thoreau had spent a night in 1849. The house was still standing and in good shape, repaired and cared for by its present owner. In Thoreau's time it was the home of John Young Newcomb, an old man in his late eighties whom Thoreau called the Wellfleet Oysterman.

"This is where Thoreau spent the night of October 11, 1849," Parker said. Thoreau had just come to the cape, traveling by train, the stagecoach, and then walking, accompanied by a friend.

"It was really his first night after the day of walking, where he had been walking along the beach. As it started to get later in the day and near dark, they decide to find a place to stay overnight, he and his walking companion. And they move inland in this area, which was all then devoid of trees," Parker said.[8]

"There was no forest, so this was open land, and they found this house and knocked on the door and were able to spend the night here," Parker explained. I looked around. Although the house was in good shape, the forest was encroaching on it, pitch pines and small oaks growing where there had been a lawn, some close enough to the house to touch it when the wind blew their branches.

"They were invited in by John Newcomb," Parker continued. "He was a ship master who had done some oystering in his life and was 88 years old when Thoreau arrived here. And his wife also was here and she 84. Once taken in by them and settled down, Thoreau was very delighted by the Wellfleet Oysterman's stories. He had stories that went back to the American Revolution, and, of course, Thoreau was interested about that. Growing up in Concord, MA, he had the Revolution as part of his background. "If you look at the house you will notice it has kind of a bowed roof here and it was actually built by shipbuilders," Parker put in.

Thoreau wrote about himself as a solitary person who didn't really like company or society very much, and much preferred to be by himself in nature. But that wasn't really always the case. Often, he enjoyed people. This was especially true when he was on Cape Cod and visited the Oysterman. Many pages of his book on Cape Cod are devoted to the conversations that he had with the Oysterman. He liked down to earth people who were straightforward, and who had contact with nature in one way or another ––– like Parker, or Murray Buell or Heman Chase. He didn't like false society or artificiality, but when he met up with somebody who was a real character and had interesting things to say, he was a very sociable and jovial.

I had brought along Thoreau's book, *Cape Cod*, and opened it to the passage where he describes his visit to the Oysterman.[9] "The old Oysterman had told us that many years ago he lost a `crittur' by her being mired in a swamp near the Atlantic side east of his house, and twenty years ago he lost the swamp itself entirely, but has since seen signs of it appearing on the beach," Thoreau wrote. "He also said that he had seen cedar stumps `as big as cart-wheels' (!) On the bottom of the bay, three miles off Billingsgate Point, when leaning over the side of his boat in pleasant weather, and that that was dry land not long ago."[10]

Trees once grew where now was ocean. According to the Oysterman, the Cape was not stationary, the very land on the Cape moved. This idea intrigued Thoreau. He wrote that another person "told us that a log canoe known to have been buried many years before on the Bay side at East harbor in Truro, where the Cape is extremely narrow, appeared at length on the Atlantic side, the Cape having rolled over it, and an old woman said – `Now, you see, it is true what I told you, that the cape is moving.'"[11] The idea that the land surface of the Earth was dynamic was novel at that time. More prevalent was the belief that life and its local environment — oaks, bayberries, the soil, bedrock — were fixed, and created a permanent, static setting. This duality continues today in our 21st Century, with some believing nature is constant except for the destructive things people do to it. Others side with Thoreau (even if they haven't read his works) that nature is dynamic and always changing. Our world today is deep into this kind of debate, which neither side ever wins, but each side makes up its own stories about how nature works.

Thoreau did not simply accept the Oysterman's and the Old Woman's stories as true. As he continued to walk east and north on the Cape, he reached the Highland Light where he talked with the lighthouse keeper. A few days later, after Parker had had to return home for other business, Ted and I arrived at the lighthouse and Ted set up his tripod and camera and began filming. The Highland light was a landmark in Thoreau's time, just as it was for us that day, a classic white pillar rising above a white building on the edge of a picturesque dune, high above the beach and the water, facing to the east, to the open Atlantic ocean. It sat on the edge of an undulating landscape of dune grass, shrubs, small oaks, and pitch pines, a mixture of patches of grasslands, shrublands, and salt-spray-stunted, open woodlands. It was a lonely but picturesque landscape. From the lighthouse, the dunes fall away steeply for a long distance, and the edge of huge dunes provided us with a grand view of the shore below. Far below, at the base of the dune on which the lighthouse stood, people strolled along the strand, tiny toy figures to us.

The Lighthouse was built in 1798 to provide one of the major lights to guide ships away from dangerous shoals along the coast of the Cape, and it performed that function during Thoreau's time. But on our visit, the lighthouse was automated and no longer had a keeper.

To Thoreau, the lighthouse keeper was a different sort of expert from the Wellfleet Oysterman and the Old Woman. The lighthouse keeper had lived and worked at the lighthouse 60 years, a length of time that amazed Thoreau. Like the Wellfleet Oysterman and the Old Woman, the Lighthouse keeper had observed the erosion and movement of the Cape. "According to the light-house keeper," Thoreau wrote in his book, *Cape Cod*, "the Cape is wasting here on both sides, though most on the eastern"[12] – the eastern shore being the ocean side of the Cape at this location, confirming what he had heard from the Oysterman and the old woman.

But Thoreau did not leave things at that. He did not accept the opinion of the Oysterman, the old woman, or the lighthouse keeper without tests of his own. At the time, the Highland Light stood back from the edge of the dune a distance that Thoreau said was 330 feet.

Having worked as a surveyor, Thoreau improvised surveying equipment so that he could make measurements. "I borrowed the plane and square, level and dividers, of a carpenter who was shingling a barn nearby," Thoreau wrote, "and using one of those shingles made of a mast, contrived a rude sort of quadrant, with pins for sights and pivots, and got the angle of elevation of the Bank opposite the light-house, and with a couple of cod-lines the length of its slope, and so measured its height on the shingle."[13] He observed that the dune rose 110 feet "above its immediate base" and 123 feet above mean low tide. Next, he checked his measurements against those of other land surveyors. "Graham, who has carefully surveyed the extremity of the Cape, makes it one hundred and thirty feet," he wrote.[14]

Then he looked for signs of erosion. He found evidence of erosion about a half mile south of the lighthouse, at the point of highest land in the vicinity. There along the dune he saw streams "trickling down it at intervals of two or three rods" which left erosional shapes like "steep Gothic roofs fifty feet high or more," which were at one location "curiously eaten out in the form of a large semicircular crater."[15] Ted and I found similar features on the edge of the dunes near the lighthouse.

Still not content with the *opinion* of the lighthouse keeper nor the measurements he was able to take himself, he examined data kept by the lighthouse keeper. "We calculated, *from his data*, how soon the Cape would be quite worn away," Thoreau wrote.[16]

Thoreau made additional measurements when he returned to the Cape the following summer. "Between this October and June of the next year I found that the bank had lost about forty feet in one place, opposite the light-house," he wrote.[17] From these observations he concluded that the Cape was wearing away about six feet a year. But he was cautious about simple extrapolation and generalization from a few observations. "Any conclusion drawn from the observations of a few years or one generation only are likely to prove false," he wrote, "and the Cape may balk expectation by its durability."[18] This skepticism — even about one's own measurements and observations — is one of the important features of science and of scientists. Thoreau was in this way very different from the intense public debates about environmental change and people's effect on nature and on themselves that we hear about over and over again. Each side of the belief — that people are changing and destroying the environment or that this cannot happen ---- are rarely as thorough and careful as Thoreau. There are many recently published articles on each side of this issue that are casual assertions often with little if any factual basis, just what are passed off as science, but are often mythical story telling.

From the observations of local experts combined with his own investigations, Thoreau began to generalize about the dynamics of the geology of Cape Cod. "On the eastern side the sea appears to be everywhere encroaching on the land, "he wrote. 'Not only the land is undermined, and its ruins carried off by the currents, but the sand is blown from the beach directly up the steep bank."[19] From what the local expert, the Oysterman, told him, and from what he heard also from the keeper of the Highland Light, and also what he learned from his own measurements, Thoreau began to understand that nature was dynamic.[20] He actually acquired the data that he needed to move beyond what seemed plausible to reach a deeper understanding of nature. He was able to reach this scientific understanding and to apply science while at the same time he was the person who, like Parker Huber, visited and revisited the Maine Woods and many other New England landscapes, searching for and finding that inner and outer contact with nature, that sense of renewal, a spiritual as well as a scientific understanding of nature, that Parker had talked about while we were canoeing the Penobscot in the Maine woods a few weeks before.

Why didn't people who had deep beliefs and feelings about nature (I'm not talking here about the scientists, but ordinary people) find it simple to make such simple measurements today, in our much more technological era, the information age, I wondered. Why were we so often missing out on the obvious? Thoreau's homemade transit on Cape Cod and his travels in the Maine Woods seemed, at least in Parker Huber's way of phrasing it, to have the seeds of an answers. Maybe it was because he had that deeper feeling about nature and sought to experience it directly, inner and outer, rather than treat it as a political issue viewed from afar or an administrative task to be completed as part of a bureaucrat's assignment, that he was open to such measurements. Thoreau's experiences, as he wrote about them in his journals and books, did seem to suggest a key to approaching the problems that surround us. His ideas and feelings seem to fit in with what Sun-Tsu had written more than two thousand years ago about the importance of measurements, and what Thomas Jefferson had written to Meriweather Lewis, and Lewis himself, along with Clark, had followed in their travels across the American west: measure, measure, measure, immerse oneself within nature.

I thought once again about what Parker Huber had said from the canoe on the Penobscot River. "I think you're traveling for the unexpected, and to just be here," Parker replied. "You don't really have to go anywhere. Matter of fact, we could just camp some place and wait for it to happen, whatever that might be. You wouldn't really know what it would be, but something would happen, and we would certainly bring us a further understanding of ourselves in the natural world. It takes a great deal of patience to be a naturalist." A patient naturalist observing closely, seeking to discover himself and nature, and making measurements.

NOTES

---

[1]. The kit, *What Makes us One*, is available from me, directly. Because we had to have it professional recorded and the DVDs and CDs professionally made, and packaged professionally, we have to charge a small amount for each kit.

[2].David White's formal statement about this research project was sent to me as an email, and it stated:

Subject:
Date: Tue, 12 Jun 2001 20:42:59 -0400
From: "D. C. White" <dwhite1@LION.MAIL.UTK.EDU>
To: dbotkin@silcom.com

CENTER FOR BIOMARKER ANALYSIS
University of Tennessee
10515 Research Drive, Suite 300
Knoxville, TN 37932-2575
865-974-8001, FAX 865-974-8027
Dwhite1@utk.edu, MILIPIDS@AOL.COM
June 12, 2001

Dr. Daniel B. Botkin, Director
Center for the Study of the Environment

1505 Crystal Drive # 831

Arlington, VA 22202

703 413 1481

FAX 703 413 1484

dbotkin@silcom.com

Dear Dan,

Good to hear from you. As usual I am struggling to maintain a research program.

Should your dog drink from the toilet bowl? This is a more serious problem than it may appear as many areas of the world fresh potable water is in very short supply. Proposals for dual water systems in which potable water is separated from gray water and used in toilets etc. A hew and cry erupted as dog and cat lovers worried about the health of their pets who regularly drink from the ever-convenient toilet bowl.

It turns out there are two major types of Gram-negative water bacteria. The Pseudomonas- type bacteria found in potable water systems are opportunistic pathogens and the really bad guys like most human serious pathogens (Plague, enteric pathogens like Salmonella and Escherichi coli. Gram organisms contain lipopolysaccharide (LPS) on their outer coat. Carbohydrates cover the surface and they are held in by lipid A which glues the LPS to the bacterial greasy membrane. The lipid A contains fatty acids which become extractible in organic solvents after mild acid hydrolysis (1). Water biofilm organisms like Pseudomonas have 3-0H 10:0 and 3-0H 12:0 as the fatty acid components of LPS-lipid A. The enteric (fecal derived) bacteria and most Gram-negative human pathogens contain 3 0H 14:0 (2). Even the most fastidious toilet bowels cleaned daily contain a biofilm at the water air interface. You cant feel it or see it but it is there. Which type of bacteria does it contain fecal or water based bacteria. In work supported by the National Water Research Foundation contract WQ1 669 524 94, Human feces contained in mol% ratios of 7 (0.6)/19 (4) 3 0H 10 +12/ 3 OH 14:0. The toilet biofilm contained 72 (30)*/19 (4) of 3 0H 10 +12/ 3 OH 14:0 LPS fatty acids [* (mean (SD)] So the toilet contains pathogens to water organisms to enterics of 0.37 compared to 3.8 in the feces. It is safe High flush and low flush did not make much difference except tha the higher the flush rate the healthier the bacteria in the biofilm.

1. Parker, J.H., Smith, G.A., Fredrickson, H.L., Vestal, J.R. and White, D.C. (1982) Sensitive assay, based on hydroxy-fatty acids from lipopolysaccharide lipid A for gram negative bacteria in sediments. Appl. Environ. Microbiol. 44, 1170-1177.

2. White, D.C., Stair, J.O. and Ringelberg, D.B. (1996) Quantitative Comparisons of in situ Microbial Biodiversity by Signature Biomarker Analysis. J. Indust. Microbiol. 17, 185-196.

Thanks very much.

Sincerely,

David C. White, M.D., Ph.D.
UTK/ORNL Distinguished Scientist

[3].. The story about Lee Talbot's experiences in stopping the use of the poison, 1080, against coyotes, is based on an interview with him over several years, but primarily Interview on Lee July 27, 2001.

[4].. CEQ 3rd annual report (1972; 1971 was Cain committee: The Advisory Committee on predator control,)

. P. Kalm, Travels in North America: The America of 1750, 2 vols., trans. A. B. Benson (New York: Dover, 1963).

6. Huber, Parker, author of *The Wildest Country* and an expert on Thoreau's travels. Personal communication during this canoe trip.

7. The conversations in *Thoreau's Transit* are direct transcriptions from the soundtrack of film taken by Ted Timreck.

8. Transcript of film made by Ted Timreck, # 02:00:39:02 – 02:03:11:28.

9. This next section is taken directly from Botkin, D. B., 2001, *No Man's Garden: Thoreau and a New Vision for Civilization and Nature*, Island Press, Washington, D. C.

10. Thoreau, *Cape Cod*, Moldenhauer edition, p. 120.

11. Thoreau, *Cape Cod*, Moldenhauer edition, pp. 120-121.

12. Thoreau, *Cape Cod*, Moldenhauer edition, p. 118.

13. Thoreau, *Cape Cod*, Moldenhauer edition, p. 118.

14. Thoreau, *Cape Cod*, Moldenhauer edition, p. 118.

15. Thoreau, *Cape Cod*, Moldenhauer edition, p. 118.

16. Thoreau, *Cape Cod*, Moldenhauer edition, pp. 118-119.

17. Thoreau, *Cape Cod*, Moldenhauer edition, p. 119.

18. Thoreau, *Cape Cod*, Moldenhauer edition, p. 119.

19. Thoreau, *Cape Cod*, Moldenhauer edition, p. 120.

20. End of material taken from *No Man's Garden*

www.ingramcontent.com/pod-product-compliance
Lightning Source LLC
Chambersburg PA
CBHW051439250726
48655CB00001B/131